Other books by Robyn Bridges:

Medicine Books

Moose Medicine: Healing Wisdom from the Natural World
Two-Legged Medicine: How to Become
Your Own Brilliant Therapist
Turtle Medicine: The Art of Swimming Sideways

Poetry

This Way to the Kiva: Poems for The Journey Home
The Good Earth: Canyons of Gratitude
Uncharted Sorrows: The Incandescence of Loss
Safe Passage: Eyes on Sunrise

———

Upcoming books by Robyn Bridges:

The Power of Place: Seduction and Belonging
This Divine Moment: Weekly Meditations for the Evolving Soul

WATER FOR THE DESERT

A Template for Evolutionary Change

Robyn Nygumburo Bridges, M. Ed.

BALBOA.
PRESS

A DIVISION OF HAY HOUSE

Balboa Press books may be ordered through booksellers or by contacting:

Balboa Press
A Division of Hay House
1663 Liberty Drive
Bloomington, IN 47403
www.balboapress.com
1 (877) 407-4847

Print information available on the last page.

ISBN: 978-1-9822-3486-7 (sc)
ISBN: 978-1-9822-3487-4 (e)

Balboa Press rev. date: 10/14/2019

*How odd that although change is the one
flowing constant in our lives,
we fight it so much.*

*How fortunate, that even through resistance itself, we
might receive both magical and ordinary invitations
to navigate the waters of those very changes.*

CONTENTS

INTRODUCTION

Shock

How do you make sense of a senseless loss?

You might assume that a seasoned psychotherapist would have pretty well learned how to flex with change. She would also have met and banished her own demons enough to be adept at navigating the landscape of loss. After twenty-five years of providing counsel and doing my own personal work, I too made the same assumption. But, following retirement, I met a completely unexpected waterloo and lost my way, falling more deeply into the mysterious unknown than ever before.

For any of us, dark nights of the soul can strip our egos and challenge whatever beliefs we have constructed; they require a deepened spiritual intimacy with change and the willingness to allow the emergence of a new template. For me, an unsettling and unwelcomed loss was drifting me into a deep void. The need to deal with the disturbance it created in my psyche rendered the situation nonnegotiable, where plummeting through and then finally letting go might be the only way to survive and invite a deeper nourishment to breathe.

The loss precipitating my own dark night was not that of a beloved person or valued career (although I'd experienced those, too) but rather of a long-cherished *place*. The startling loss of vibrant relationship with a deeply meaningful place might be similar to waking up one morning with a jolt after years of familiar *human* companionship and wondering, "Who *is* that person sleeping next to me, and why are we together?" In the absence of my own human partnership, a few favorite sacred places had become confidantes, companions, and lovers. So, upon returning to the once-enticing Sonoran Desert after having loved, keenly needed, and relied upon it for so long, imagine my surprise when I felt *nothing, nothing,* wondering why the spirit that used to water the desert landscape, delighting and hydrating my soul, was now absent, gone without a trace or even a whisper of a goodbye.

Who knew it could even be possible to experience such destabilizing loss of relationship with a *place*? Who knew this loss would catapult my former capable self into a shock so deep as to render me parched and immobile, thirsting for the sustenance upon which I once depended?

And who knew this would ultimately forge a channel for evolutionary change?

 # WEEK ONE 

Chapter 1

Everything Begins Where We Do

THE THIRD DAY

I am returning once again to the Arizona desert, having assumed I will re-ignite the same passion I have known of this welcoming place so many times before. In the past, I have sought it out during bouts of frightening personal change and loss; in response, the desert has always revealed itself in all its glory and majesty like a lover, ready to take me in. It has romanced me and I have responded with eager delight. I have been able to literally slip inside the familiar natural world of plants, animals, land, and sky like a shamanic artist, feeling the energetic essence of their benevolence and soaking up lively spiritual sustenance. As a result, no matter the emotional or spiritual need, I have found stability, encouragement, and renewal.

So now, with child-like anticipation, my old SUV and I have just rolled into the verdant Sonoran Desert for three months to escape another frigid Montana winter. Surely, I will once again be embraced by the faithful Saguaro Cactus, sturdy Mesquite trees, and sandy pink boulders. I will imbibe the desert's fragrant offerings and commune with a wise group of invisible beings I met here many years ago whom I have named "The Ancestors." Because of my unplanned and sometimes unwelcomed solitary life, I have learned to lean deeply into special geographical places that I perceive carry spiritual nourishment. Until now, I hadn't realized how deeply I have depended on them. I am unaware of any great inner change afoot on this visit, simply excited but at ease to return, blithely imagining that all will be the same. The landscape will be welcoming, as always, and the spiritual beings I've come to know and love will envelop my eager presence.

But as I drive through the first familiar stand of Saguaro Cactus in the rolling foothills of northeast Tucson, something has changed. Glimpsing the dark orange desert sand and massive pink-hued boulders, I feel separate from it all, as though I'm viewing a one-dimensional painting whose soul I can no longer crawl within. It is a new and unwelcomed feeling, like meeting your self and having it not recognize you anymore. I cannot reach into the once-sentient desert or feel it greeting me as it used to. I can't hear its lively, gritty voice or feel it communing with me deep in the cells of my body as it used to, nor can I appreciate desert colors or textures. I hear but am numb to the cardinals and cactus wren chirping as they explore the tall Saguaros, and I don't smile to see the Mickey Mouse-shaped ears of the short Prickly Pear cactus as I once did.

It feels too quiet. Dead, even. Or maybe I am dead. Breath catches in my chest. The upper portion of my heart feels like a concrete slab just fell on it. The lower part seems entirely absent. I am slightly embarrassed to be having such a strange reaction, although no one else is around to witness it.

What is happening?

Now I start to worry if I'll even be able to access The Ancestors anymore, who, in the past, have seemed to reside at a nearby seasonal and sacred waterfall. Maybe they have disappeared, too. I call out to them through the open windows of my moving vehicle but my words fall to the ground. My mind freezes. Even in the lingering warmth of late afternoon, a slight shiver runs down my spine.

I just assumed it would all be the same. Assumed. That was my first mistake. I had no idea how dismantling their absence would be.

Am I in the right place?

There is no sense of my spirit meeting theirs, no delight in hummingbirds flitting by or the Cactus Wren singing, no way to make this one-dimensional desert deepen.

Still driving, I hardly feel that I am in my own body at all. I don't know where "I" am or even *who* that is. Feeling the unexpected loss of spiritual connection to the desert, I begin to tentatively seek help from a type of consciousness that I have come to call my "Inner Teacher." I am not even sure I can access that wisdom either, but I have to try. Otherwise I'll be living in a banal place, disconnected within and without, unappreciative and unaware, unable to access the great gifts of spiritual relatedness I've known so well. And that is no life at all. My life has become too rich on the inner planes to settle for banality.

As the sun sets, I drive up the final short hill at the edge of the stately Santa Catalina Mountains to my condo. I hastily unpack and gravitate to the private back porch that opens out to the revered Ventana Canyon. I unceremoniously plunk my tired self down in an old Mexican wheeled rocking chair. Still in shock, I sigh, blandly gazing around at lengthening shadows covering the mountainside army of Saguaro Cactus and spreading Mesquite and Palo Verde trees, and, slowly rocking, begin to ponder.

What has happened? Am I in a bad dream? I still can't even feel myself in my body—such a rare occurrence for me.

I should just be loving my small, recently purchased, quiet condo, whose private exterior overlooks and snugs right up to the open space of Ventana Canyon, shouldn't I? I look back over my shoulder through the large living room window, ruing the fact that I barely noticed or appreciated entering this fully furnished, well-stocked space a new Tucson friend so lovingly prepared. I had spent months prior to my arrival commissioning coral-brown countertops and alder wood floors and selecting hand-carved Mexican mesquite tables and chairs; I purchased a ridiculously expensive leather and fabric sofa and decorated once-lonely walls with original desert oils, carvings, and artifacts. All was arranged through many long-distance phone calls while I remained in Montana, recovering from a long illness. Here I am, finally, healthy again, and I must say that even in my altered state, it looks beautiful. After much fussing and a slimmed-down savings account, my nest is complete.

But I am not. Something is amiss. So, I do what any good addict would: I go to the nearest grocery store and come back to eat sugar, drink wine, and go to bed.

After a restless sleep, I pad out to the back porch the next morning and begin rocking in the large Mexican chair. As the sun rises, it reveals more contours of desert mesquite and Palo Verde trees with every inch of increasing light, but I am not sure if I am part of that light. I am not really here. I know my body is feeling fine rocking back and forth, but my emotions and spirit seem to have vacated. They must be nearby, but, nevertheless, it is very disconcerting. I am not used to feeling out of my own self. I used to wonder about people with mental illness who would claim they were hardly ever in their bodies and seemed to know that state well. Now I can relate to them and to James Joyce's description of a certain Mr. Duffy, who "lived a short distance from his body." I say it aloud with both a wry laugh and a worried frown. That is me now.

My body rocks, yet my psyche remains still, hanging out somewhere else that I can't quite reach. I don't know when I left my body or when I'll be back. It might have been somewhere along the thousand or so miles traveled between here and Montana; maybe it began even earlier, during the mad preparations for this six-month sojourn.

I don't know who is breathing this body. I want to trust that this is all part of the plan (whatever that is) but wish someone had given me advance notice. I don't like change that I don't choose. Between arguing and pleading with God for information about this odd and unwelcome event, I fall silent and absent-mindedly gaze at the sun rising. Breezes tickle the tan grasses leaning against the desert rocks that lie patiently just beyond my back porch. I wonder what that would feel like, to be met by another energy, even by wind, and to be affected by it—because nothing is affecting me.

Expressionless, I listen to the little birds with loud voices and the big ones with small piquant cheeps and listlessly watch dull-colored hummingbirds buzz around the Saguaros. I see the blue of sky but can't feel it as I used to. It is revealing its vast clarity but I have no clarity myself. It rests on undulating lines of the mysterious Santa Catalina Mountains, a mystery that is quickly becoming my life.

I feel vaguely safe here, yet am not sure where "I" am. Though I do not feel watched over, as in years past, I know the Sonoran Desert itself is still protective by nature. Prickly Pear and Saguaro Cactus and Palo Verde trees sport huge needles eager to poke the unwary—the thick undergrowth dares all but the most qualified to pass through. Usually, these qualified ones are the native residents who, in former years, have greeted me while passing by: cougar, bobcat, havalinas (wild pigs), roadrunners, a cacophony of birds, bees, and even the occasional errant human hiking on some foolish or sacred task. My tasks are both foolish and sacred: foolish because I expect to easily renew membership with this wild community and sacred because I am seeking answers for this startling lack of connection with the landscape. I'm not feeling the presence of the group of spiritual beings I first met here so many years ago, either.

The Ancestors came into my perception subtly but powerfully when I found myself unexpectedly alone and bereft in my early thirties. Dismantled, I had escaped Montana for three months to live in the desert, loping along toward some inexplicable arid call. Family and friends had all judged me and turned their backs because of my necessary choice to divorce and be only a weekend parent to the unattached (attachment disordered) children who had come into our lives and we were trying to raise as our own. They would not or could not allow parenting or connection. Their ongoing bizarre behaviors at times involved unthinkable danger to animals, other humans, and themselves. All my naïve dreams of a normal happy family life had been dashed.

In the desert, depressed and untethered, I had been weeping at a lovely waterfall behind a nearby resort when I became aware of four or five presences hovering in the sky in front of me: long, tall, semi-opaque beings with robes that trailed down into nothing. Though I didn't see them with my physical eyes, I saw with my perceptual ones. They felt warm, welcoming, and wise. I had been feeling frightened, crying about child loss, loneliness, and rejection. How do you re-create a life when the old one has so painfully aborted? How do you experience a living death and come through the other side?

These wise ones seemed to understand. They seemed quite real— what some might call "imagination"— but clear messages were being relayed to my mind and heart. They offered encouragement, support, and a sense of being held. *Forgiveness. Empathy. Seeing the bigger picture.*

Sometimes when the human world utterly rejects you, the only place you have to go is to another realm, where you hope and pray you might be accepted—even loved.

The gifts the Ancestors so realistically offered settled right into my body, heart, and soul. I began to breathe the longest, deepest breaths I had ever taken. Even in the midst of sorrow, I could begin to feel new life surging through.

From that moment on, I knew that, somehow, everything was going to be all right.

Though I returned to Montana, in the following decades, I had often come back to the desert and walked up to the sacred waterfall to visit my invisible friends. One night, these beings even revealed the vast mysteries of the universe to me, stories of how everything began, which I later learned were called the Akashic Records. I was utterly amazed and transformed by the experience, but, like many other-worldly encounters I've had, I couldn't remember most of the specifics later.

I just know that in the moment, similar to my earlier Near-Death Experience, I knew everything about the world, the universe, our shared history, and the complete loving consciousness of all beings as One. Perhaps people who we would call "enlightened" or "awakened" embody this powerful awareness all the time. I was only able to hold it for a few moments. But I'm not sure that judging anyone as enlightened or not is really helpful; I just want to draw close to the Divine in everything by learning, growing, and living the best life I can. I feel simple and elemental in that way.

But now, thirty years later, on the back porch of my little condo at the edge of the Ventana Canyon, I do not feel simple or elemental. I feel nothing. I gaze through the branches of Palo Verde trees and around sentinel-like Saguaros at the early morning play of shadow and light sweeping across the rises and folds of this dramatic mountain range and wonder how to regain a soulful connection here. Maybe I am different now and thus am unable to access it again. I am older, and, sometimes, weary. The children who came into my life eventually left the shelter of my home and now wander somewhere in the world. I hope they are not experiencing stress or doing ill. While parenting them, I had tried, imperfectly but sincerely, to provide everything I could. But it wasn't enough. Ultimately, they couldn't attach for any length of time to anyone who tried to parent them.

They are a sad and tender memory.

My many godchildren have grown, and though they love me, are now living their own lives all over the world, and I seldom get to see them. I have only one immediate family member left (who seems to want anonymity) and a few cousins I met when I was sixteen. I don't even remember their names or exactly where they lived. The rest of my immediate family has died.

When the last one, my loving father, passed over five years ago, I rolled through a surprising and powerful grief process over a six-month span, moving from a sense of appreciating and missing him deeply to that of sore abandonment; these feelings eventually morphed into a sensation of being adopted by the world (a fascinating experience). Yet shortly after feeling adopted—to my relief—I realized I didn't even need *that* perception; I was already a part of the world via my birth into it. I was a spiritual being who had an intentional birth. With this realization, in the following months, I sailed on the wings of Spirit while keeping my feet on the good earth. It was then that my heart, though scarred, began to heal. The resulting freedom and relief were immense. I began to integrate body and soul back into the world on my own, yet felt more deeply connected to all of life than ever before.

My aloneness began to feel sacred. Still, holidays or any event that emphasized family tore at the sutures in my heart. Being with other people's families on those occasions began to feel more painful than helpful. It would cause me to keenly miss my own family's landscape of familiar, even frustrating, camaraderie, complete with family fights and humor, favorite relatives and dislikable ones. Unable to call any of them back from the dead, I eventually retreated into deep solitude.

In truth, we are social more than solitary creatures by nature. Yet I have spent more time alone than I ever imagined I would. Though I have always known I am whole within and have learned to appreciate and even treasure seclusion, it doesn't always feel that it has been my choice. Sometimes a solitary life still fills me with melancholy.

In existential moments, I feel alone in the world.

So, I seek wisdom, here on my tiny back porch, gazing up into the morning blue, and call out for my own sky within.

I wait expectantly.

No one answers.

I purse my lips and push my breath out my nostrils like a toddler not getting her way but too afraid of her strict parents to throw a full fit. I complain, argue, and shake my head. Then I sigh, come back into my adult self, and calmly ask to be taken to a place where all is explained and I find out why I never had my own birth children or a happy marriage or family, the only things I keened after and so desperately desired.

I am now waiting.

I am still waiting.

What do we do with dashed dreams? Do we coddle them, nurse them, or pile them up like grudges in the closets of our victimization?

I don't want to visit those disappointments anymore. I want to live now, in the present, feeling beauty and breathing in the possibility that resides in every moment. I want to choose new perceptions to fill me with the peace I seek.

So, I turn my attention to my Inner Teacher, the engaging encouragement I have received on the inner planes so often in the past, asking it to teach and reveal, both through the drama of the Ancestors at the waterfall, if they are still present, and in the quiet meditative enclave of my protected back porch here and now. Everything may begin where we do, but it will leave off in the middle of a sentence if we try to push and pinch it into some form of a twisted desire. I will do best by staying open, quieting my demands, and listening.

I am still impatient for answers to why I've lived such a solitary life. But patience seems to be asked of me now. All I can do is listen, observe, and be as compassionate to myself and others as possible. To be kind and conscious. To feel gratitude for life itself. To imbibe messages from the universe by interacting with people, animals, plants, and places. To befriend my inner landscape. To remember to help others in the midst of their own needs. And to consider what trusting the process of life might actually mean.

When I drop my arrogant insistence that life be a certain way and then choose to inhabit a state of awareness long enough, showing up every morning and inhaling possibility, I just might eventually return soul back into body to once again inhabit life itself. I vaguely suspect that when I release the need for my desires to be met, they will actually have a chance to meet *me*, even if in a different form. So, I wait, this time tentatively flirting with a bit of inner quietude instead of courting angst and strife.

May I be a good and patient listener both today and every morning as each new day arises.
May I become newer, freer, and more fulfilled as a result.

YOUR INVITATION*:

1. Have you had dashed dreams? If so, have your feelings about them changed over time or not?

2. What do you need regarding those former dreams now?

3. What part does waiting play in your process of discovery?

---

* *Because I want to offer you the opportunity to be fully engaged within your own self, I offer a few questions at the close of each of these journal entries. I trust you will know whether you want to write your response, think about the questions that drew you in, or just breeze right through them! Or maybe you'll form and respond to your own musings instead.*

Chapter 2

I'm A Mess

THE SECOND AND THIRD DAY

The next morning, recovering from the thousand-mile drive from Montana to the desert, I am still secretly expecting to feel a return of the old excitement, the thrill of absorbing the scents and sights of the stately Saguaro and Prickly Pear Cactus that dot the landscape, anticipating the intertwining blend of mystery, memory, and passion.

But I still feel nothing. Nothing! How can that be? This desert has brought me alive for so many extended visits. I have returned each time like a lover, excited to breathe as one with this formerly magical place. I have human memory, too, during one visit, of a man I met here when the nights luxuriated in our presence. Human loves, mountain hikes, and spiritual awakenings through the Ancestors had safely tucked this verdant desert deep into my being.

Over the next few days, I grocery shop (more food and wine), make a few calls, and do laundry. I absentmindedly swim in the condo's community pool. But no spiritual arms (or human ones) are extending to wrap around me. No one and nothing reach out. As I gaze over the same line of peaks that once filled me with amazement, I feel as if a large, thick, glass window has been erected between the mountains and myself. I am a foreigner now, a first-time tourist, unsure of what currency could provide the sustenance I need. I remain flat-lined, dropping my jaw open and staring at the landscape.

I never considered that this land would some day seem as distant to me as a star, and not nearly as beautiful. Some people may not need to relate to special places on earth as much as I have; perhaps my own lack of personal human intimate partnership for so long has re-centered itself in intimate connection with places on earth. I've come to rely on relationships with the land as much as with other people.

Only seldom have other people stunned and shaken me as much as the land has this time. And because of it, I'm bereft. Alone. Confused. I'd be mad but I don't have enough "I" to feel that emotion. How odd. How bizarre.

However, I have discovered that the one consistent thing I can do during this time of feeling so out of my body is to rock on the back porch and greet sunrise each morning. The rocking seems primal, perhaps a return to the womb where life felt accompanied and safe, and the cooing doves and buzzing bees who increase their tempo with the rising sun help me both get out of myself and also recognize that the whole world is not out of kilter and a mess. Just me, right now.

This morning my mind is stewing and uneasy. I am irritated and unsettled. Befuddled. I want to get away from that noise in my head (matching those constant construction sounds that just started up over the hill). I hear the chorus in my mind: "You can run but you can't hide!" Ha. Damn, that song is right. *Beep, beep, beep.*

I am awash in grief over losses and dashed dreams of family and children. My mind is racing. I have been alone so long because I must be a bad person. I must be unredeemable. Devoid of any goodness whatsoever. I can't let go of my lost dream and it has ruined my life. *Beep. Beep. Beep.* What is this chattering unrest, this terrible inner judgment? Is it a replay of lessons from a critical mother, how it was to grow up with that merciless tyranny? The cadre of unseen beings I've met through the years who love me might be helping me to recognize patterns, even of that harsh upbringing, that I'm perhaps just now ready to release, but why has it taken so long? Might I also struggle when I travel to my other favorite winter escape in Hawaii? Is this angst over a non-magical connection to the land reflecting a loss of passion in general? Could that be in part due to aging and decreasing hormones? *Beep, beep, beep.*

Now, three decades after meeting The Ancestors at the waterfall, I am tipping the far edge of mid-life and still anticipate re-visiting that cascading backdrop to try to sense their presence. Once I've settled back into my surroundings, surely our relationship will feel vibrant and alive, by now more collegial than student/teacher. I will be content to just bask in their company without needing to desperately request their help.

Or will I? This sudden vacating of my body has got me wired. When will I feel at home within myself again? I have no point of psychological or historical ego reference anymore. I used to feel stable and know my belonging to places, my own quiet, and my past. None of that is relevant any longer. Who am I as related to God and where do I belong now?

I am frightened, a ship with loosed moorings that has run aground on dry soil. I have no ease of water or fluidity to greet this unwelcomed experience. I am languishing in the desert without nourishment or sustenance to see me through.

Disoriented, with no mind or opinions of my own, I wonder how I am even thinking with no mind left. Along with it, my soul seems to be gone. Where did it go? Why? How can I get it back? A deep dismantling seems to be occurring. I consider calling one of my good shamanic friends who carries true power and asking him to do a journey or soul retrieval for me; although I know how to do one for myself, there is no energy available for it. But something tells me that even in this state of not-knowing, this is a personal 'must-take' journey, one that can't and won't be rushed or 'fixed' by any known process. There may be many things I'm needing to learn that will only come from being as present as possible. It will be important to not fight the experience but to simply allow it. I don't know if this is correct or not, but it's all I can go with right now.

So, I go with it—only there's nowhere to go and nothing to do. I alternately rail at life, myself, and God and then sink into deep inner silence, where thoughts barely form and then float away. When I have even a whisper of a thought, I question how this experience of loss of place could happen without advance notice or my consent. I feel sideswiped, victimized, and out of control (and I have been used to feeling *so* competent and *in* control). I must be undergoing some kind of soul surgery to which I never agreed. My pulse is slowing. The dull thud of my heart begins to diminish until I can't feel it at all.

During the next few days, I do manage to shower, feed myself, and even interact with a few people. I think I sound normal to them. But I feel as if I'm in a slow-motion movie with no sound. I can't begin to talk to myself, let alone anyone else, about what I'm going through because I have no understanding of it. I basically rock on the back porch all day and every day.

Although I've explored and developed a powerful spirituality over the years, this is some deeper, more mystical territory I have wandered into inadvertently. This morning, I wonder about my recent intensive foray into Quantum Theory over the past several months, which claims that we, as waves of divine thought turned into particles ourselves, can truly create everything we desire from the Field of All Possibilities. Could these hours of dedicated study be prompting the many questions now plaguing me? Could they be part of a necessary dismantling of unconscious limiting belief systems to clear the way for manifesting the life I truly desire?

The new scientific findings of the neurobiology of Quantum Physics, as detailed by researchers Dr. Bruce Lipton, Gregg Braden, and Dr. Joe Dispenza, as well as the HeartMath Institute, make a convincing case that we carry the power to craft our lives through combining the power of the mind's intention with the corresponding emotions in the heart. By consciously choosing our intentions, selected from this divine Field of All Possibilities, we can actually, through epigenetic prompting, create our desired future in the present moment. I have been finding a bit of success with this, and it certainly fits with my sense of how much more magical (in the most intelligent sense of the word) we are than we normally let ourselves realize.

But right now, there is nothing I know anything about anymore. For having been so self-assured most of my life of my easy connection with God, even as it has morphed and changed, I am nowhere now. The fact that sages extoll something I imagine might be similar to this state of not knowing does nothing to ease my distress. I obsessively question, in fits and starts, who we are in relation to God. Are we God or just part of Him/Her/It? What does it mean to be spiritual beings in human bodies, really? How does that actually work? Is our humanity our stumbling block or an opportunity to dissolve seeming opposites? Is our human psyche truly a separate part of us, as is Spirit? How do we weave them together, if that is even what we're up to? Are we truly wave turned to particle by a miraculous, loving intelligence? How do we activate sentient power? Why do we need to know any of this? I have to know!

My mind short-circuits and I resume a dull staring out into the desert for hours. Once in a while, I think, "Oh, I'm just a hot mess" and feel very stupid. Not "hot" in the sexy sense of the word—just a boiling contraption of contradictions that don't fit. Yep, a hot mess. That's me, now. Or whoever or whatever is thinking this.

As the first three days of this descent into extreme discomfort jumble along, during moments of ego-awareness I feel ashamed. I am dull, inadequate, and must deserve to suffer for my stupidity. What is wrong with me?

So what a surprise that, on the fourth day, the enormity of those feelings ironically become the key to my exit from prison. I don't know who jailed me—outer or inner forces (and I think it could be either, or both)— but I begin to realize there may be a way out and that I don't need to stay confined.

By some chance (or design?), on that fourth morning of my unwelcome experience, while randomly reading a few book selections and listening to a podcast, I happen to hear about the element of choice in how we experience change. Something clicks in me. Immediate chagrin sets in. What if I'm going through whatever this is in an unconscious dysfunctional, cultural, almost self-abusive and familial way?

This is huge. The experience has been full of guilt, the familiar worry that I've done something wrong and am unredeemable. The sense of being wrong, lost, and helpless is too similar from when I was a teenager and one of my parents (I dislike parent bashing, but yes, it was my unhappy mother, who is now deceased) would corner me in my room, berate me for something I either had or more likely hadn't even done, tell me how sad it was that I was so disturbed (which even then felt untrue), and leave, closing my door ever so quietly, as though I was a sick patient in a mental ward who might crack. Crazy-making! So was I now experiencing a spiritually challenging moment in the same way, being abusive to myself?

New-Age or esoteric thoughts aside—like "these disturbances are the challenges associated with changing from the third and fourth dimensions of physicality into fifth-dimensional crystal light bodies"—all I know is that I'm suffering, with no redemption in sight. I am drowning in the mess of dissolution without solution. I am in the unknown, gasping for air, and frantic.

I shake my head (if indeed it is mine to shake) and plead to God: *I don't know what I'm supposed to be learning from all this. I have to trust that perhaps over time it will become clearer. All I know is that I can't live with this extreme discomfort anymore. So I think I have a choice here, and I'm exiting the process. I don't know if I'm aborting something that would have been better if I stayed with it, but I just can't believe that the compassionate god to whom I want to be hitching my wagon would want me to have to continue to go through whatever this is in such a grievous manner. I'm recovering my intention to do everything in alignment with my values of freedom, peace, and joy, and accomplish them all with two of my favorite words: GRACE and EASE.*

A few years ago, in a moment of sudden insight, I had realized that the qualities I absolutely wanted to live with, day-in and day-out, were freedom, peace, joy, grace, and ease. When I first had that epiphany, I went about telling all my friends, enthusiastically listing the qualities on each of the five fingers of one hand. I was so full of relief and recognition, along with an undeniable joy, that my friends who were also steeped in consciousness tended to get excited, too, a few of them realizing, clarifying, and naming their own deepest spiritual values. Now I was remembering Grace and Ease as the two companions whose hands I might take and walk out of this bleak existence.

Although this dramatic descent had probably been brewing for a couple of months, in part from my intensive study of Quantum Physics, the actual dramatic decline has only taken three days. *Three* being the universal spiritual belief of the time from death to resurrection does not escape my wry thoughts. While I will stay alert to possibly continuing the quest of questions about God, I will now choose to do so in a kinder manner.

With a thrill of relief and a sharp in-breath, I can feel that I am choosing to walk away from trauma. I am glad to keep learning and keenly want a breakthrough, but to maintain any sanity, I'll have to release both the war and the content. I prayerfully ask to be made aware of everything I need to learn about the subject of my discontent (how are we related to God, what part do we play, how does that actually work) but in alignment with my values of Grace and Ease.

Exhausted, I shakily step out, an act of volition based on a desire to survive in freedom rather than a mental institution.

A few hours later, nothing much is materializing, at least not in my cognition. I'm not sure what is happening in my heart. I do feel sadness in having to leave a huge topic like "how are we related to God" unfinished, but am also starting to revel in a palpable relief of some kind of shy and newly found freedom.

THE NEXT FOUR DAYS

During the next four days following those daunting three, I take a few swims, cook some good food, and put my bare feet on the desert floor. I ask the earth to forgive any myopic attitudes I have had about this shift in relationship with it, and assure it I love all of the natural world and am willing to connect with the desert the way things are now, without holding it or myself to some disappointed standard. So, I begin to sing an impromptu song of appreciation for all the desert's rock, plant, and animal inhabitants and the pinky-red soil itself. It seems to offer relief. Or is my relief offering itself to *it*?

All in one week, seven days—an experience of biblical proportions, but still no ultimate revelation.

Slowly, I begin to feel that I am inhabiting my body more often. My soul and healthy ego seem to be tentatively piecing themselves back together. I am now alone in a new way. I feel a bit of peace as I resume morning meditations, noting various rocks along little trails leading off my back porch. I pray to the earth, the sky, God, Goddess, and the Universe, offering myself to each. In a more detached way, I am rehydrating in the desert, my ribs filling as do the Saguaro, swelling with nourishment for the next dry spell. I swim almost every day. I begin to luxuriate in water.

I am feeling different. Better. Almost like a new person. Like I had a cellular facelift or organ replacements. Even with that, I still don't understand what the vicissitudes of the descent were or are all about, which I pray to discover in the coming days. I sometimes wonder if I sidestepped true enlightenment because I was not willing to stay with the awful feelings long enough. The content seemed valid: a deep quest to understand more about the nature of God and humans. But the manner in which I was handling it might have been self-defeating. The chagrin I felt in realizing how unconsciously I'd been repeating the pattern of abuse turned inward was enough reason to gather my volition and step out. I actually like that my first reaction upon loss of the desert relationship was to try to draw closer to God. But the manner in which I experienced it was like my upbringing, born of the power of negative familial and cultural conditioning.

Bits of the big picture are now slowly coming into focus. What if there is something in my deep unconscious connected to everyone else's and this bizarre experience of not knowing myself anymore was exactly my part to explore in order to consciously participate in the progression of unknown? What if each of us need only respond with open hearts to whatever arises, trusting it is necessary to bring us in alignment with the larger whole and catapult us into our next phase of evolution in a more brilliant, compassionate, won't-blow-the-whole-world-up kind of way? What if this actually is what esoteric wisdom and New Age philosophy claims, that we are moving from the third dimension of the physical to the fifth dimension of less attachment to the way we've been, thus making way for a new, more vibrant perception of who we really are?

Before this loss of all sense of self and ego, I'd never really been interested in the question of who I was; since I was very small, I just knew I was a little earth girl, come straight from heaven yet right up through the earth, here to experience the joy of life and to praise creation. That's all I needed to know, as over the years I busied myself in nature, my constant companion. As an adult, I busied myself with how the human psyche heals in the natural world as I sought to help others recover from their own traumas, in similar fashion to how I had been finding success in my own healing. It had been the heroine's journey for sure, as scholar Joseph Campbell outlined that vast territory, ranging from hearing the call, to descending, to finding the gift and returning to one's village to share this gift. Only my way felt more distinctly feminine, with less bravado and more intuitive knowing.

On my conscious journey, I've also experienced a place I would call a true void. Each void has been unexpected and different from the ones before. One void came about from a deep meditation during a Transpersonal Hypnotherapy training that catapulted me into pure emptiness. It was daunting but felt purposeful, like building soul muscle to tolerate the unknown. It only lasted an hour or so. Another void brought me into a more comforting sense of the unknown, as though sentient beings were surrounding a somewhat existential sense of nothingness. That one lasted a few months, during which time I continued to see clients in my private practice while to all outward senses carrying on a "normal" life, even though the inner was unsettling.

Yet another subtler void lasted almost a year, seemingly prompted from a Native American event. It began with a lovely ceremony, connecting several lessons I'd been given by representatives of the Wolf Teaching Clan of the Seneca Nation. I remember when Grandmother Twylah gave me the name "She Who Knows the Way." I was surprised and honored, but also secretly a bit ego-inflated. "Oh, I guess I'm really *something*," I thought, followed by a nervous inner giggle. But in the next moment she admonished, "If you aren't already living up to these qualities, you'll become aware of their opposite and the truth of how far you have to go."

So, of course, that following year I completely lost my way in the world, quite humbling for a psychotherapist. I felt utterly untrusting and bereft of knowledge, self-compassion, the ability to help others, or the capacity to utilize any navigational skills. And this was after years of helping others! However, through prayer, meditation, and contemplation, followed by an exhausted surrender from "My Way" to "The All That Is," I slowly recovered and did resume a life. I discovered something important about the cyclical nature of everything. Like the circularity of the Medicine Wheel, we go around and experience all of the facets of whatever we are going through. In the future, if the same subject is triggered, we begin to circle around again; yet each time we go around, we do so more quickly, with a little more alacrity, a little more ease, and a lot more insight. When we cycle fast enough, the issue actually morphs into infinity, and it is no longer "an issue." It is alchemized from our sight, our lives, and our hearts. The dross may not even remain as much of a memory. The gold is that our energy is now freed up to experience whatever else life or our souls offer. This could be a model of how evolution itself works.

After my experience of that particular void, I did inexplicably begin to return to the reliable structure of inner wisdom and the connection between my psyche and spirit. During several future Medicine Wheel workshops that I conducted in the sweet tipi on my property, I told workshop participants that story, admitting that during the "lost" year I had to rename myself from "She Who Knows The Way" to "She Who Hasn't Fucking Got A Clue." That always elicited a round of laughter, the sounds of palpable relief from participants as they would realize I wasn't someone sitting above them in any way. I was just like them; I simply had a few helpful systems I'd learned that could assist them in working through their own muck, too. Because of how I'd learned to traverse the Heroine's journey, I could once again hold space for them to deepen, move through, and free up their own lives.

I'm retired now and don't run workshops or offer individual or group retreats anymore. That energy used to build up in me if I didn't move it through often enough, which meant I was pretty busy offering healing work. Over the years, a few of my own teachers had affirmed it was the same for them. I wonder if what I've gone through lately is that same energy building up in me again, but when not used, it ferments. It may want and need an outlet. I will put that out there into the airwaves and see what might open up, trusting what does or doesn't happen as sufficient and correct for me. That kind of relaxed response is new for me, and welcomed, although I also giggle to realize that this writing itself may be the offering.

Writing about the void has helped me feel like less of a mess right now. Or maybe just more comfortable in *being* a mess. Paradigm shifts are seldom easy or neat, and this one is no different, if that is indeed what it is. I am in the deep unknown. Can I befriend it? Is it befriending me?

I feel better having written about this. Thank you for listening (you can bill me later). I hope and trust that there is something from my path that will support you as you journey on yours. We are all seeking happiness and wellbeing, aren't we? Maybe some souls are here to progress and evolve (like mine seems to be) while others want to just float along the surface and not do battle with inner demons, or maybe simply do not have as many to slay! Who am I to judge one way as better than another? No matter our intent, we still get to love what we love and be attracted to others we might term "our tribe." I love my tribe of seekers who are steeped in the principles of Transpersonal Psychology. These folks explore beyond the small self into the vast expanse of direct spiritual experience with discernment but not judgment; they carry a signature form of kindness and compassion. We often recognize each other instantly, sometimes even hugging after a short interchange. *Ahhh....*

My life has been so solitary, and somehow magnified when I keep traveling all over the world. I think I may need to find a group or conference soon to feel the collective heartbeat of that love incarnate once more. Who knows? If you are one of my tribe, we might even meet at a soulful gathering in the near future!

May I remember that there is goodness everywhere, even in the midst of my own mess. May you and I know we are more than our despair and open to self-compassion, and that we can move through the void into a new beginning that will reveal itself organically. Meanwhile, may we take heart knowing that just as we are all in this mess together, we might also be a natural part of the cleanup!

YOUR INVITATION

1. When have you felt overwhelmed, confused, and in a "hot mess"?

2. How did or can you get out? Or is that even the central question? What *is* the central question of your life?

3. What purpose might be served by getting lost? What did or will it take to return with gifts for your village?

WEEK TWO

Chapter 3

Learning to be New

Even though I am recovering, I am still a bit shaky in the world of psyche and spirit, not knowing what my current relationship to the desert actually is. Faithful to my morning back porch rocking, I gaze out at the Saguaros dotting the mountainside and the Palo Verde trees spreading their leafy branches and just wonder—about them, about life. In the absence of any new relationship, I am free now to turn my attention to other things amiss in my life. I have what I call a bit of "free attention" when not overcome by the shock of last week. But where do I put that free attention? To problems I wish to solve? Maybe there is a gift in this moment if I can just stop complaining and explaining my angst to the universe. It knows it already. Why be repetitive? With that reminder, I fall silent and come alive to the moment, not only to the one unfolding in front of me as the morning shadows creep across the boulders at the edge of my porch, but also to the corresponding place within, perhaps leading me into some new territory to which my perceptual eyes have never before been opened.

Staring at the shady rather than the light side of the Saguaros, however, I fall once again into familiar past sorrows. Childlessness. Lack of family. Deep disappointment that seems to suck the breath out of my lungs. I am lost once again. How do any of us avoid being trapped by difficult past memories? I would like to avoid the places of bad memory; I want to enhance the good. But as I gaze across the desert canyon landscape, I realize that both happy and sad memories can lock me in a vice. If that is all I allow, think of all the possibilities to which I am saying, "No"—because I don't even realize there can be anything else. Or, I am afraid to have new experiences because that to which I am accustomed feels safe, even if it prevents optimal living. Old habits die hard.

This morning I am surprised to feel an opening to wonder itself as a possible new friend. I immediately decide to activate my power, and looking into the blue sky, and declare my intention aloud: "I experience abundant health, wealth, and relationships." But then, after setting intentions, even as a beginner to this application of Quantum Physics work, I know that I must next surrender it all to the Universe and befriend the unknown, living as though I already have what I want before it has even manifested. So, I surrender to the outcome. Relief stretches through my body as I feel the edges of a new willingness to take a chance and move forward. In the light of a fresh new morning, and in a moment of surprising returned energy, I am considering flying before knowing if I yet have wings.

Unabashed, I feel into the wing attachment on the back of my shoulder blades at the exact moment a small brown bird with a light peach-colored breast appears and hops around the gate of my back porch. He flutters and my shoulder blades respond. I note the synchronicity and court a quiet intuition that certain New Age as well as ancient esoteric teachings are rooting and manifesting in my mind, body, and soul. And certainly in my direct experience.

These teachings say that this increasing sense of the unknown so many of us are experiencing runs concurrent with the crumbling of civilization itself; it feels like the end of the world as we know it because we are in the middle of a radical shift from third to fifth dimensional human capacities. They explain the third dimension as being our current physicality, full of opposites and limitation. The third dimension is now re-capitulating through the fourth dimension, which serves as a transition into the fifth, where we develop crystalline light bodies with which to soar in expanded states of bliss and wellbeing. We peel through the old and are made new in body and spirit. As "out there" and daunting as this seems, the "symptoms" they tag as being signposts that this is actually happening are rather convincing: demise of the patriarchy and immoral power, the return of feminine empowerment in both women and men, mass exposure of government and personal corruption, world-wide wars, individuals and groups banding together for a higher purpose, a sense of impending doom, a personal clearing out of past history that is holding each of us back, and increasing spiritual realization of our primary unity and spiritual benevolence. During this time of demise, they admonish us to look up and in for the help being offered by sentient unseen beings. They tell us we will become new in the process. We will become unified. Smarter. Fluid. Similar to my own life-long vision of Heaven on a new Earth. Can we release fear of approaching change, embrace the unknown, and dwell in the new with open hearts?

Can I?

I look up to the pinkish-brown rock-studded mountains right in front of me, who carry so many secrets I may never know. Or could I? If we are co-creators with the Great Creator (the very issue with which I've been struggling: what part of God am I, and what power do I really have?), can't we know everything, as I did momentarily so many years ago, right here in the desert when the Akashic Records were revealed to me?

I want to know everything, and, of course, I want to know it now. I give an impatient rough rock in my chair, my heart and soul keen to know all the secrets of the universe—right *now*!

However, I am most keen to understand more of what I've just been through the last few days, which I am certainly not through yet. It still feels disconcerting, and even though I have chosen to release myself from the pressure of having to work it all out, my mind is still restless. I want to understand everything, in part to just be done with this excruciating inner journey that somehow found me, dragging me along while I protest and pull away, without even the decency to provide a map of where we're going! (A bit of righteous indignation raises its head.)

And just then, wouldn't you know it, I am given a clue. A large, cat-like animal suddenly comes into view, ambling around the corner toward me along a narrow path to my right between the outside wall of my condo and large overhanging mesquite trees. I can't believe my eyes. He appears to be a young, healthy-looking bobcat, his back a desert brown, chest and inside legs white with mottled black spots, his ears sporting tiny black tufts. He is sleek and sure of himself. He seems a bit surprised to see me but keeps coming. He briefly sizes me up while I slow my rocking, but he keeps laconically moving at a slow pace right by my little back porch, glancing at me from time to time. Too soon he disappears in the shrubs while I sit in amazement.

Then he's gone. Did that really happen?

After I remember to breathe again, I have to Google the spiritual meaning of Bobcat. Why, then, should I be surprised to read that such a sighting (Bobcat "medicine") is primarily about patience? Patience and the importance of awareness.

"Oh," I sigh to myself. "Okay. I'll just chill with the timing of everything. I'll stay aware of whatever comes into consciousness as it arrives." The message feels firm and wise, so I remind myself that I can act like a mature astrological Aries who has actually learned how to both watch and wait, allowing life itself to unfold in its own good time.

In the next moment, my peach-breasted bird friend with the tiny beak reappears, alighting on the metal porch railing and then hopping around the concrete floor; I assume he stayed somewhere safe while Bobcat was gracing the area. He is unbelievably cute, and clearly more of a ground-hopping bird than an insects-in-the-tree-hopper. I grin at him for a long time. He often tilts his head and looks up at me as he hops around my chair. I gaze at his effortless being, laughing to myself that he doesn't need any of these thoughts about life and meaning with which I am struggling. I remember indigenous people, who claim that animals are actually more developed than we are and are just waiting for us to catch up. I giggle and decide that if that is true, I'd better get on with my own consciousness until it has once again re-sculpted my life so I can then release it to the greater good and become more like him. As if he takes the compliment, the little bird fluffs up his round chest and confidently settles on the cotton rug in a corner of the porch, clearly comfortable staying close by as I ponder.

My heart is slowly opening to my thoughts, seeking a way in. But I am pretty sure that it is supposed to go in the opposite direction: our minds are meant to be directed by our hearts. Heart is to direct the mind, not the other way around. It reminds me of what I'd been learning from teacher Gregg Braden about the science of the heart being even more powerful than the brain. I still feel somewhat foolish that this recent falling apart has happened, but at least now I can breathe through it a bit more so I can return to sorting through my pressing thoughts, which still seem important. I am trying to piece a life back together, allowing the demise or morphing of old beliefs. Who are we without belief systems?

I am beginning to feel my heart a bit more. I remind myself that when mind and heart connect, miracles happen for anyone who applies certain principles. Published results from Quantum Physics researchers are measurably and scientifically astounding. Both instantaneous and gradual healings of desired outcomes have been thoroughly documented and celebrated by those learning how to activate their newly realized divine power.

To allow ourselves this "newness" returns me to my Wolf Clan teachings about the Medicine Wheel. We always begin in the direction of the East, the place of new beginnings, infused by spiritual direction and divine imagination. Everything is still forming in this place, the unknown incarnate. We release fear and instead learn to breathe in the excitement of these new beginnings, choosing to deepen trust that all is well and in alignment with a greater plan. Maybe I can allow both ancient teachings such as these and corresponding scientific discoveries such as Quantum Physics to integrate into my understanding and light the way to a new and better way of living. Perhaps I can also choose trust over doubt and ease over angst. Then I might more easily release the past as I ready for fresh adventure, allowing life to unfold and my soul to be both initially challenged and ultimately enhanced.

As I begin to accept these ideas, I breathe deeper and my ribs relax. A wiggle moves my hips. I feel fluid. When I surrender to a process like this one, of actualizing a desired future, I begin to actively link with Spirit and a sense of higher good, moving with the fluidity of water into the unknown with my typical earthy curiosity. Even though the principles of Quantum Physics can sound heady and complex, as I imbibe them I ironically become willing to spend more time not knowing than thinking that I know anything, because unexamined assumptions quickly become old perceptions.

While deciding to believe in my own power to create, I simultaneously surrender and allow a new present to form from an imagined future. I am reminded that whenever I expect my present to be confirmed by my past, I am limited in all that I could be experiencing and all I could become. Yet when I expect and feel my present showing up as a chosen future, I begin to experience cellular change matching an aligned heart and mind. I then take a well-founded chance and befriend change. I let the old dry up and dissolve and the new to form and nourish. Today, I am learning what part of the divine I really am and a bit of how to access water for my own desert, here and now.

The bobcat returns two more days in a row. Patience. Awareness. I've got it. New qualities. I take them to heart.

He doesn't return again.

I am new each time I find the courage to release attachment to the past. This allows me to fly into the territory of the increasingly friendly unknown.

YOUR INVITATION:

1. What keeps you stuck in the past?

2. How do you react to change, a need for patience, and the "unknown"?

3. How do you access water for your own desert?

Chapter 4

Breaking Out of Self-Made Prisons

Three weeks into my initial shock of losing my connection to the desert, I am, of course, still rocking each morning on my tiny back porch. I gaze through the protective metal gate defining the porch boundaries out into the boulder-strewn land stretching before me. The shadows are already fleeing from the sun, receding from the various pink and brown jig-jag canyons all along the lovely face of the Santa Catalina Mountains. With surprise and relief, I am pleased to realize I am appreciating their beauty in a new way, even if I can't relate to it the way I had before. I'm just letting mountains be mountains, and sunrise be sunrise—always beautiful, even if I can't crawl inside them anymore.

This morning I am sensing the hint of slight openings to a world where freedom and joy surround everything, feelings I have not had in the slightest during the last two weeks.

It is daunting to admit the walls I've built. Walls against feeling too much or experiencing unsettling changes. Walls against allowing a new intimate relationship with another human, not just with places. Walls against relaxing into the not-knowing of things and trusting the sacred to have my back.

For all of us, our job, perhaps, is to practice staying aware, from moment to moment, of heaven itself weaving through all we think, say, and do. No small task, because our human dilemma seems to be how to navigate through the world of perceptions that have been overlaid by experiences in which we have drawn protective and, sometimes, needlessly narrow, negative conclusions. Maybe our souls choose to go down dark or lonely roads, greedy or cruel, but I wonder if even those choices are just that: choice. When we realize we can choose freedom and love in every moment, letting go of the past, giving and receiving, we might live joyous lives full of greater wonder, possibility, and welcome. Lately, however, my consciousness has been arrested by the lack of welcome in this desert experience. With such recent shock and resistance to feeling no connection to this rich place, have I been locking myself in a prison from which only I can free myself? Do I then berate myself for that ignorance?

Everything has its own season.

If self-made prisons are constructed from belief and perception, are they so deeply ingrained that we are seldom even aware of their form or how they are constraining us?

I think of people I know. A struggling young mother hesitates to ask for the help she could be receiving from a local agency. An elderly man doesn't accept visitors in his home because they make him feel lack when they leave. A body-worker ignores her own physical needs as she compulsively tends to others. We so often don't realize we are in prison at all! But once we do, can we allow the friction of chagrin and discomfort to carve a new pathway to be watered? When we open, so do the floodgates. We remember to breathe again and become glad of it. In the process, we become more willing to release our ego's story and attachment to how it has formerly known itself. This is likely what has been frightening me, but for me to live in freedom is to be willing to allow the experience of change itself to be freed from the resistant and judgmental prison to which I have relegated it.

Prisons of my own making become evident when I continually grieve the losses I've had. When triggered by past memory, I blame myself, God, or others for the misfortune. And when I see it as misfortune, then a whole host of assumptions follow: "Because this happened, life is hard; I'll never get what I really want; I've been forgotten; I don't matter; I've done something to deserve this; I'll never be free." Wow. That is quite a litany of prison bars that will keep me stuck in the same place until I allow my perceptions to change. I am finally learning that perceptions create assumptions, and assumptions create our reality. It really is that powerful, and that vast. It has taken years to begin to recognize the bars of prisons of my own making and to dismantle them. But each time I do, more fresh air surges in and I stride out into a vast landscape, full of the unknown and pregnant with possibility, if I am only courageous enough to keep walking.

It could be that the current prison of my own making from The Descent of late (which is so hard to consider because then I have to take responsibility for all of this being up to me and not someone else) has been resistance to the apparent loss of spiritual support and companionship through the power of place. This loss of a connection feels as valid and real as the loss of any human relationship. While the other person in a human partnership can walk away, we seldom think of a place as doing so. And yet, might this loss of relatedness with the desert actually have been prompted by my own higher self to allow this fond old connection to die for reasons that I don't yet (and might never) understand?

My consciousness has surely been arrested now. Currently living an untethered retired life, I have little else to do but contemplate and allow awareness its due. I read, I rail, I sigh. Even the metal gate on my back porch suddenly looks like prison bars. This is such an inside job (ha, I see the irony) that I have nowhere else to go.

The late astute philosopher, poet, and author John O' Donahue writes about being in prisons of our own making; his writings are surprising and shape my own thoughts. His inspiring book *Beauty, The Invisible Embrace* sits open on my lap today. In it, he reminds us of our natural freedom—not that we have to work to develop it, but rather, that we must work to dismantle the bars we have erected against it. This can be a life-long process. Freedom arrives from the gift of consciousness (certainly delivered through our Inner Teachers). Consciousness is the revelatory mechanism provided so we can experience the sentient values for which we most long, as well as learn what is keeping us from them.

As I consider how much I am currently still living in a prison of my own making, it helps to remember to allow my more objective observer self to view the situation from a higher vantage point. First, I see myself as a young seven- or eight-year-old, pouting, with crossed arms. Of course, I always want what I want. Don't we all? But as we age and begin to gain glimmers of wisdom, we might consider a greater plan we could trust, just as we once effortlessly trusted our bodies to grow and change and mature. Could something greater be at work in a sentient unconsciousness with me now, only unconscious and problematic because I am not yet willing to be aware of or surrender to what it wants to teach?

My wiser, older self is standing nearby. I see her in the shadows, tall and serene, waiting to come forth when I am finally willing to consider shining a light on all of her contours. I suddenly breathe in very deeply. Something unexplainable has shifted in me, but it is good. The dance between what I think I need to be doing and something greater effortlessly working through me is syncing up.

As if in response to this allowing, the desert's morning shadows finish dissipating, retreating from the sun's full face. The mountains stand in the light, bare and beautiful. I sigh, and it suddenly occurs to me that there is no reason not to open my back porch's metal gate with its many bars, open it to the sun and desert and all the creatures that might come by, or even come in! How long has it taken me to realize there are so many great freedoms offered to us, both within and without that we so often ignore?

When I am afraid to step into the unknown, to take a chance, to stop fighting and trust that something better will become apparent, I suffer needlessly. I am often surprised to discover a prison of my own making and that I was carrying the key in my assumptions all along. The more I open my heart and mind to a broader and kinder consciousness, the more keys fit into doors that swing open to a more compassionate and lovely life. I am stepping into the waters of a new life even in this first moment as I think of more completely letting go. I am considering it.

I open the gate.

I see possibility.

I become freer with each moment I am willing to open.

YOUR INVITATION:

1. What self-made prisons have you experienced?

2. How did you— or do you— release yourself from those chains?

3. Who or what has taught you to begin to find your freedom?

 # WEEK THREE 

Chapter 5

Monkey Mind

With the unwelcome loss of the spirit of Place from my desert sanctuary, I seem more susceptible to a worried and restless "Monkey Mind." I so dislike that term; I can't believe I'm even referring to it. I see it as a derogative slur on monkeys, something that says more about our inability to truly understand the species than about any intrinsic fault of theirs. When we use it to describe ourselves, it implies that our minds are erratic, frivolous, and a mistake, something to twist, disapprove of, and change. With the possible exception of how our knees have been constructed, I think we are pretty much exactly the way we're supposed to be.

Yet if the term "Monkey Mind," according to popular definition, suggests the brain as full of incessant, unrelated inner chatter, it does actually seem to fit my state of mind this morning. Amidst the onslaught of half-finished, wildly unrelated thoughts chattering away and irritating me before I'm even out of bed, I arise pre-dawn, and, grumbling, toss a light shawl over my shoulders and pad over to the back door. With a strong kick of my foot, its stubborn squeaky hold yields. Taking in the dark shapes of the sleeping mountains, I begin to breathe slower. I am once again ensconced in my favorite place, ready to rock outdoors.

Until the sun actually rises, and while the light of dawn slowly breaks, I rock and return to thinking a thousand different half-thoughts, which thankfully begin to fade in the half-light of morning.

Until they do, it's "the groceries, when will I get back to my diet, what was that weird dream last night, why are they so bland lately, will I go get another plant for one of my tall pots today—did I measure the diameter properly? Why couldn't my sister and I have ever made peace, how (but I never felt her to be a sister anyway), sad, oh, here comes the sun, what a precious moment, let me not miss it..." While a small part of me is actually realizing I sometimes like to let my mind roll, the larger part is aware that this is also how I lose precious energy that I would rather be using to focus, organizing meaning into understanding and letting myself be taught by the wisdom of consciousness itself.

Thankfully, thoughts quiet down as the rising sun draws my attention to nature. Shadows appear in contrast to the light spread across the undulating line of mountains in front of me. I hear doves cooing, welcoming both each other and the day. Quail bob along dusty trails, weaving in and out amongst the pink and gray "Stone People," an indigenous name for the lovely rocks who dot the land. Saguaro Cactus surreptitiously creep up ridges, but with each moment of increasing light stand revealed in all their serene nakedness. The eastern side of their bodies slowly become fully illuminated while their western flanks remain gently shadowed. Next to them, several large-needled Palo Verde trees capture my attention, looking soft at a distance to my aging eyes as they form a blurred backdrop around the Saguaro sentinels. I carefully nod to nearby Prickly Pear cactus standing staunchly with their spiked and rounded Mickey-Mouse ears, ready to poke any unwary passersby. Chortling, I remember how they have had their fun with me more than once.

Loosely focused on nature now, I return to gazing at the changing patterns of light. I am absorbed by beauty. "The gaze," as philosopher and psychoanalyst Jacques Lacan declared, is powerful, because "only there is where we exist for one another." Does the Saguaro gaze at *me*? Does it exist only because I gaze at it? Or do I exist only because it gazes at me? Regardless, it is through "the gaze" that we behold the Beloved. In that gaze we *are* the Beloved.

At least that was my cursory understanding of a college presentation on his work that I heard years ago. Though I felt incredibly stupid for not understanding more of the technical jargon, I was still moved to tears, so I tentatively approached the speaker after her talk to express my gratitude, dropping my chin while confessing how little I understood but how deeply it affected me.

She smiled brightly. "You've got it. You don't need to be able to banter semantics with the academics here. Some of them never allow themselves to feel what you're feeling. It went straight to your heart, which is exactly where it was meant to go."

I bravely met her eyes. With my chin now tilted up, I thanked her, and raising my rib cage, let myself saunter out of the lecture hall.

The Gaze. We all have it. We feel it in our solar plexus, our hearts, at the back of our minds… It emanates through our eyes during moments of profound reverie, dawning realizations, and keen regrets. Most pleasant is the contemplative gaze of utter stillness, where thought is suspended and space opens for love to unfurl. We engage with it in so many ways: the look between lovers, the eyes of a pet, the moment when for some inexplicable reason everything in the world seems just right, the quiet satisfaction of breathing in the present moment.

This type of gazing is not an absent-minded way of staring when actually thinking about something mundane; rather, it is a volitional entering in, a purposeful beholding and reflection about something deemed significant, whether visible or invisible. In those moments, full of gratitude, we reciprocate the heart and soul of creation. Mystics from the twelfth century, Rumi and Hafiz, described "the gaze" as the way the Beloved beholds itself. They both knew the gift of a relaxed mental and quiet, focused consciousness, the same that many of us do in our present days.

But attention can be hard to sustain. I begin to feel how many different tracks my thoughts are starting to follow. So, before my undisciplined Monkey Mind cleverly swings me off track to grab at the branch of a diversified intellect instead of the divine moment (sorry, monkeys), I quiet myself, breathe in, and return to gazing. I don't want to miss a moment of receptivity to this gift!

The notion of focusing on the natural world beckons deeper. A butterfly warms itself on the desert-colored overhead wooden beam supporting the far edge of the porch. My hummingbird friend flutters briefly only a few inches in front of my face. Looking out, I breathe in the dusty green of desert plants. Doves chortle and flap as they land on telephone wires strung high above the porch. While I don't like the wires, I welcome the doves. I think they're the same ones who have been alighting overhead for a few days now. If I am quiet enough, I won't disturb them. Though they glance at me, they soon turn their backs, quiet themselves, and soak up the first rays of sun. They seem to be gazing at the changing light, too, just as I am. It is still quiet, and I think they like that as much as I do. Somehow, I intuit that, for them, the quiet is everything. And I imagine that although they hear the exquisite chortles of other birds, sounds of distant traffic, buzzing insects, and small animals scuttling in the underbrush that I might never hear, right now, they—like me—are primarily absorbing the gentle beauty of this new day. My mind now quieted, I breathe in the rhythm of sun, of plant, of air. This could be a path through the shock from which I am still recovering, a loss to beat all losses, unplanned and bizarre.

Just now, may any unfocused thoughts
diminish as do shadows from light.
May "Monkey Mind" slow to make way for your awareness
to arise as does the sun. May you let out a long sigh
and focus your gaze into the heart of sentience.

YOUR INVITATION:

1. What is your connection to the term "Monkey Mind"?

2. What restores a quiet balance in your mind?

3. What does "The Gaze" suggest to you?

Chapter 6

The Bird Clan

This morning my eyes are barely open and my body still half-asleep as I attempt to move by rocking on the back porch. Though I continue to recover from the shocking loss of relationship with the desert, I can feel that I'm still in the middle of a dismantling and reconstructing process. I can also feel that I am not breathing very deeply, nor do I want to. I *harrumph* to myself: Why don't I breathe deeper? It is so healthful to do so. After all, I've taken four years of intensive Breathwork training and taught it to others for fifteen years.

With sleep-laden vexation, I remember that, yes, we probably teach what we need to learn. I feel some resistance as I tell myself to breathe deeper. Maybe it was one of last night's unwelcome dreams I'm recalling. Or one I can't.

However, my mood begins to lighten as early morning shadows shorten, matching my breath; I laugh to feel justified in merely being the shallow breather I am today. I think about how lucky I am to have the questionable privilege of moving through this odd rite of passage of losing "Place" or whatever has been happening, while I remain unhindered by work or other responsibilities. Or does it make it harder because nothing else is demanding my attention?

I chuckle about all these thoughts and how sincerely I am trying to sort everything out, feeling a bit of self-compassion for being the mental maven that I am. I hear a bird chirp nearby, making a similar gurgling sound. It is then that I begin to notice a variety of lovely birds alighting on bushes near to me, prompting a memory recall.

Years ago, at one of my therapeutic Breathwork trainings, I reported to the group that I had spent an entire two hours during the ensuing music and deep breathing just hearing, seeing, and feeling the flapping of wings and smelling their powdery fragrance. Usually, this type of Breathwork brings up all kinds of personal history to be cleaned out. But this one felt bizarrely welcoming and ceremonial. It was the strangest Breathwork I'd ever experienced. One of the participants, a rather shamanic-like woman from Norway, told me that the content signified that I was being formally welcomed as a member of the Bird Clan. Though surprising, it also immediately made sense to me. I had been honored for my love of all birds, the ones I'd saved, the ones I'd protected, and the ones from whom I'd received helpful messages over the years.

I liked that. I still like that. For some time, I have practiced the shamanic approach of asking permission from various birds to slip into their bodies with my awareness, and upon feeling their agreement, emotionally and physically feel my way on in. Their ways of being are astounding, and such a privilege to experience. Sometimes I can also simply call in the birds to come close by sitting up straight, opening my heart, and finding the somatic feeling in my body that matches their vibration. It's hard to describe, but I know when I've got it. And every time I do, birds begin to show up.

So, this morning, I turn my attention to the birds flitting around. But ironically, as soon as I do, they disappear. I feel tightness in my chest. What is going on? The outer is lack of birds. The inner is lack of breath. I move deeper into recall of the wonderful gifting of the birds from my Breathwork. I let their powdery smell fill my nose. I remember all the times I've saved birds—fallen from nests, slammed into windows, out of the jaws of my swaggering cats. I feel in my body what it is like to soar on an updraft of wind, to return to the nest, to blink a liquid eye while watching prey. The hawks and eagles cascading along the slopes of the Madison Range in Montana, the Great Blue Heron at my favorite private lake, the Sandhill Cranes jumping in circles as they strut their mating dance for each other, the first Meadowlarks of spring searing out their clear call from old fence posts along miles of ranch roads—all of them crowd my memory and flutter my heart open. It is then that my breath effortlessly deepens, and I am reminded that the natural world always offers a way back to our most relaxed and content selves. Though I am in the desert now, and have been deserted by the spirit that used to inhabit this place, the winged ones I know best have all gifted me in my long-time Montana home. Maybe it is time to befriend the bird clan here in the desert with more attention and affection. I need to give them a chance.

I return my gaze to the desert in front of me, focus on the energy in my heart, and simply feel into the local birds' vibration that I'm hearing but not seeing. I whole-heartedly hop, as it were, into their energy field, and emit a silent call. *Ahhh...* at last. Within a few seconds several of them pop back into view, some alighting in the Mesquite trees and Palo Verdes nearby. Chance? Could be, but I do a little experiment just to see. I immediately turn my heart and attention to something else, and within a minute, they are gone. Then, once more I focus all the love I can muster toward them, in utter humility knowing it is not I who control the birds but the law of attraction acting upon us. And again, they return within moments, staying longer now to preen and watch the surrounding trees, chortling as they sing morning along. I preen a bit, too, tending to my own feathery hair, and settle in along with them, now ready to live this day as any natural avian-human would.

I am so grateful for this capacity. Surely, we all have it; some of us may just have realized it more than others. St. Francis of Assisi certainly had this blessing in much greater measure than my own. But then again, more or less doesn't really matter in the vast scheme of creation, does it? I catch myself making this comparison, which springs from my ego, and remind myself to align more completely with Spirit. I know that to compare and then judge clips my own wings. The more I simply allow what is, the more I feel welcome both in my own human culture and that of the birds. I want to live this way. I want to both walk the earth as a two-legged and to fly free.

This is the only medicine I need today. It is brief, just a momentary up-draft, but enough to take off. I soar.

I find my freedom when I slip into the body of a bird.

YOUR INVITATION:

1. Is there anything keeping you from an experience like this?

2. What is your sweetest connection with animals?

3. What has your connection helped you to do, know, or feel?

Chapter 7

Don't Hate Me for Being White
(or, at least, forgive me)

I have no idea how or why certain topics are coming to me these days in terms of order or content, but I have no energy or desire to fight them. So I don't. I just have to trust that each topic that arises for my attention is asking to be scrutinized, cleaned out, or just loved and accepted for what it is. Although lately I feel a steadier psychic recovery from loss of relationship with the desert making headway into my cells, I am still not at ease with this new unknown territory and feeling so out of control on the inner planes; I am still not inhabiting my body regularly. It is as if I wing for a while and then, *whoosh*, I'm gone again. Wouldn't it be nice to think that angels are taking these out the very parts out of me that are needing to be re-arranged and then placing them back inside?

I actually had that happen many years ago during another trying juncture in my life when I had just moved to Boulder, Colorado, home of hippies, bliss bunnies, and wise souls. I awoke in the middle of the night to perceive five or six long, tall, kind translucent beings lovingly pulling invisible pieces out of me, discarding some and re-arranging others back into my body. All I remember is groggily sitting up a bit and mumbling, "Oh, thank you, thank you so much," before falling back to sleep.

I wish I could know that something similar is happening now, but I've had no such experience so far. I have to remember to just breathe through each moment and be as kind to myself as possible. So in an effort to take a psychic break from my still-kind-of-weird state of being, I have been reading what I thought would be a light-hearted book that a friend recommended. She meant to help me let go for awhile from my constant beseeching about this strange "no place" that had come uninvited into my awareness, the void that arrived after loss.

Perhaps since I am so deep into the territory of loss, my own history with Native America is arising. A friend who knew I was in a profound state recommended this book as "a beautiful and light read." This morning I have just finished it, and it is indeed beautiful. However, it is anything but light-hearted. Kent Nerburns' moving story, *The Girl Who Sang to the Buffalo*, is a captivating and I think true account of his experience as a white man in Indian culture, where many natives deeply distrusted him. I have experienced that, too, with some First Nations people happy with me and others not. My own teachings some years back as an honorary member of the Wolf Teaching Clan of the Seneca Nation, with Grandmother Twylah as my elder, invited me into a native spirituality full of admonishments to listen to animal wisdom, align with the energies of the earth, and treat all life with respect. Grandmother's own grandfather, and his before him, had a vision of what they called "The Rainbow People," of all races and beliefs blending into one colorful whole. They saw that actually the 1960's Caucasian generation (mine) would need to amalgamate all spiritual teachings worldwide in order to come into the kind of unity that would keep us from destroying the earth and each other. Though I heard that some other Seneca clans were not happy with her for opening teachings to non-natives, within our little protected Wolf Clan we were nurtured on the meat of living a life balanced in the natural world. This way of being was already familiar to me through my own Celtic roots, African drumming, and personal discovery, but to have received her specific teachings and encouragement for what I already instinctively knew was a great gift. I loved being with her and her family and the ancestral wisdom they shared and taught.

Reading Kent's descriptive, compelling book has activated personal recall of the relaxing vast magic of the natural world, particularly as seen through Native American eyes. It reminds me that to breathe in fresh air wafting scents of trees and flowers, soil and water makes the start of any day a good one. My spirit often yearns for quiet and open expanses, or sometimes the shelter of a deep forest. Anywhere plants grow and birds fly, where the silence of the day speaks loudly, is good. I am probably very native in that way; I'm sure some Native Americans might tell you that is one of the few ways. But, still, when I experience a native person's anger at me for being a white representative of all that is evil, who ruined their culture, I collapse. I truly am deeply sorry for my ancestors' atrocious actions. I am aghast at what "we" have done to their culture. Yet I know in my bones that I have been native before. It has been a central guiding encouragement in my current life. "New Age crap," some of them have said. But I have had so many ancestral, spiritual encounters and actual un-embodied voices who have guided me to specific earth sites full of native energy and synchronistic events that I know my connection is real. I know what I know. When something that powerful has been revealed and makes your life better, fills it with meaning, and provides inspiration to live well, what is the problem? Is Spirit culture-centric?

Still, books like Kent Nerburns' tutor us white folks (and other non-Indians) in the art of what we don't fully understand and the importance of proving ourselves trustworthy. Learning differences of perception, values, and action between Native and Caucasian cultures can be both surprising and valuable. The power of Native spirituality is a true living force of which, even with all my amazing spiritual experiences, I am sure I have only touched the edges. I often sorrow that I was not brought up in a culture that was still intact with the natural world, Spirit, and one another. What a gift that would have been! From my years as a university Native American Studies Teaching Assistant, I became steeped in the history of white domination, learning about all the horrid things we did to a people so deserving of respect. I began apologizing all the time. But I also got to a point where I realized that "white guilt," though perhaps a necessary first step, needed to morph. Even as I moved through that phase, I was guilted many times by angry Indian people for being white. Kent, in his book, was even more targeted and a frequent recipient of suspicion. Though a person of integrity, he was held guilty, disliked, and distrusted by his native contacts. He hadn't done anything overt to earn those reactions, yet he kept apologizing and bowing his head over and over. I wanted to hop into the book and redeem him! I wanted to say, "Yes, we were so awful. Many still are. But let's be aware, let's apologize, let's listen, and still move forward!"

It gets old. No forgiveness. No redemption. I lie down in the bitter gall, until I release myself and say, "Enough!" What more do I need to do? I am weary of being the beating board of another culture's anger at my own culture's admittedly horrible and ongoing trespasses. But I have also been the recipient of reverse discrimination (of course not to the disastrous extent of the decimation of entire Indian cultures) and experienced frequent snubbing. If Indian people want to express the beauty of their peace, where is it in those moments? How can I express peace myself, even in the face of their anger? What do I still need to see and understand? What do they?

How do all of us truly heal our past and create healing for the present and a template for the future?

Of course, our government needs to do more for Indian nations. I would think that Indian people, too, will continue to ask collectively for what they need and non-Indian, especially Caucasian, government and individuals should respond. Perhaps then we Caucasians might someday earn the same measure of respect that Indian people want from us. But when will white culture have paid enough? When will our apology be truly given and accepted? When will mine? I don't even attend public Powwows anymore because it feels like many who attend are saying, "Look at us, what we have. Admire it, but don't come too close. We'll let you in on just one of our dances, but the rest is for you to look in on. You will never be one of us." Especially after the time I spent with members of the Teaching Lodge of the Wolf Clan of the Seneca Nation, to feel shunned like this makes me lonely and sad. Hopeless. It stops my breath. I want to become one with everyone. At the same time, I also breathe a sigh of relief realizing that the desire to be in unity with all peoples is not anyone's exclusive cultural value!

Though I tend to be very critical of my own Western Caucasian culture (both its actions and its values), I do hear those of other cultures who see its gifts, which are sometimes also available to Indian people. But perhaps it is too hard for their entire culture to receive from "my" culture when it offers money but at the expense of soul, where there are still many invisible barriers and differing values, and they are understandably too wary from the history of mistrust through broken treaties, both then and now. I just tire of the same negative generalizations toward me from another culture whose past I admire and whose values I seek to embody.

"I am not the enemy!" I want to cry out. Though of course, unconsciously, in certain ways I am, guilty of all that another culture might point to that resides in my own culture's shadow. Although I attempt to increase my awareness and make amends where possible, sometimes I see more of the gap than the closing of it.

One thing I know. My spirituality, my wonderful and magical encounters with wildlife, sacred places, some native peoples, and the "Grandmothers and Grandfathers", spirit beings who have lovingly taught me, are true. Native culture has so much of inestimable value to teach Caucasians, but we must find a way to bridge the resentment so we can truly open our hearts to one another and enhance all of our lives.

But this morning, even gazing at the lovely play of shadows and light, I see only edges and boundaries, including my own separation, and cannot find my way through to the unity and peace I desire.

*May I do my part to enhance unity and deeply meet
my brothers and sisters of another culture.*

May we all become trustworthy to ourselves and to one another.

*May we meet at the peace table to intend
and realize a common good.*

YOUR INVITATION:

1. What has your own experience with another culture involved?

2. What sense have you made of it?

3. In what ways does or doesn't your soul fit into your own culture and its values?

WEEK FOUR

Chapter 8

Silence

During these early mornings, just before dawn and on into sunrise, I love listening to the silence of the natural world. I'll hear an occasional coyote cry or an owl hoot, and unfortunately, always a bit of hollow reverberation from traffic down the hill on the main road, but I let those distant sounds flow into and out of me like the chords of a guitar. They are here, then gone, as ultimately, I will be, transported into a state of heavenly quiet. Silence is the handmaiden to the eternal.

The soul is always rebalanced through silence. It calms the worried mind and slows the busy body. It is rich with information not easily accessible to the everyday human rush. It is truly the vibration which animates everything, the "pause between the notes," as poet Rilke described. When deeply listened to, silence contains a quiet assurance from the universe which soothes the existential heart.

At first, silence can feel threatening because you may become more aware of fear, separation, angst, bad feelings about self or other, or negativity in general. But if you breathe right through those feelings and are willing to either work with them to heal or just let them pass through, you may discover that silence can befriend you. You come to realize that the discomfort from the verbiage of negativity has been a defense against the intrinsic quiet beauty from which we originated. To recover a friendship with silence may require initial courage, but shortly after, the once-fearful soul will find a welcome and sustainable relief.

Now I move deeper into the inner world of silence. It helps me to sit with whatever I've been avoiding and find how graciously it can be attended to. In this way, listening to silence is an opportunity to befriend our eventual death. It is the precursor to the vast choir of the heavens, a reminder that we are only here on earth for a short time. That is as it should be. It is helpful to be reminded, even daily, to cherish the time we have here, as well as to enjoy the relieving lack of clatter and clutter whenever possible. Silence: to some, water for the thirsty soul. To others, the great gaping unknown. Because it subtly mimics death, at least to our frightened egos, it is also understandable that so many avoid it.

I love how silence stretches; because I so love it I become greedy for it. I want it to last forever in my heart and mind. Somehow, it expands my thinking while relieving my weary brain. After a time of no thought at all, it often leads me to ponder the big questions about past, present, and future. Could all three timeframes be actually happening at once? New Age philosophy and even some quantum physics theory might say that there is no time per se; it is a construct. But personally, I like living in the current perception of time as finite. I think I'd go crazy trying to be aware of all the lives and dimensions in which we might all be living at once, with past, present, and future personal and universal events happening simultaneously. However, lately I've been having memories of other times and places while synchronicities are occurring in present time. My ego rocks a bit with each of these experiences. They feel de-stabilizing, and I have worked so hard to create a stable life.

I have friends who can manage this time-warp awareness. But the way I've known myself up to now says, "Not me. I am a simple earth girl. I came up out of the soil in this world, this universe, and this space and time." By the same token, however, I also relate to the argued existence of ancient civilizations of Atlantis and Lemuria, and even find shared, surprising "historical" memories and connections from those places with some people I meet. I don't know how to hold all of these seeming contradictions within until I drop back into the gift of silence itself. There, nothing seems to be at odds. Everything is held in its vast expanse.

So, this morning, I breathe out all possibilities, experiences, and realities into the wide sky. My soft, round, apricot-bellied little bird friend alights on the boulder right next to my porch with a quick, squeaky call. He is looking for food and doesn't seem to see me because I am so still. Then he notices my fingers moving on the keyboard and flits away, warning others. But they ignore him and come around anyway. Soon, even he must have gathered back his courage, because he returns and hops closer to me once again.

I breathe in gratefulness, watch the avian visitors briefly, and on the outbreath, return to focusing on the deep quiet "nothing" of silence. As the sun begins to light up the mountaintops and catches my eye while gracefully spreading its fingers of light down into the canyons, I again take a long intentional breath to shift my attention into a deeper quiet.

Silence. Stillness. Nothing. Everything. I allow my eyes to open and close as they wish. My body relaxes and I am no longer "I." I have left ego behind and have morphed into the essence of what must be the mind of God. The mind of us all.

I stay in this awareness as long as possible, letting my mind rest in a happily altered state. No thought, no concerns, just being the silence itself. Often, during this time, I feel incredible joy, amazement, and alignment with absolutely everything. It stretches into infinity, as do I… *Ahh…* If only we would remember and let ourselves be renewed by this gift more often. *May it calm our hearts so our spirits can sing. May it quiet our minds so we can take appropriate action in the world. May it open our hearts to forgiveness so we can live in greater peace.*

These prayers must live in the spirits of all who give over to the manifold gifts of silence. And where better to do so than outdoors at the dawn of a new day?

> *Let us cherish and benefit from a vast silence*
> *within and without today. May we thus live our*
> *lives in the quiet hum of universal alignment.*

YOUR INVITATION:

1. What are your most profound experiences with silence?

2. Under what circumstances are you likely to avoid it?

3. What does your Inner Teacher want you to know about silence?

Chapter 9

It's All Perception

The morning sun has just popped up over the eastern ridge, and two greenish-brown large lizards are frantically chasing each other up and around rocks a mere ten feet from my porch. I don't know if they're fighting over territory or a mate or food. Finally, one reluctantly skitters away, and the victor scales a boulder, proceeding to arch his impressive scaly green body up and down several times, his dark eyes darting back and forth, kind of like Rocky at the end of a fight scene.

I laugh, but I wonder, was that all pure reptilian instinct or did these animals have a choice of how they could have perceived that incident? Botanists and biologists would surely say "NO!" to the latter, but my imagination of what is possible has always stretched beyond the boundaries of science. The lizards looked for all the world like they were enjoying a drama of their own choice and creation.

I have often thought it could be hubris to claim that humans are the only ones able to choose perceptions through the vehicle of what we call "consciousness." With the indigenous respect I have learned from ancient teachings about animal wisdom, how do we really know? All I know for sure is that we humans do have choices of what to think and feel according to how we perceive a situation. I begin to wonder how blind I have been to the various ways I might be perceiving this new loss of relationship with the desert. I thirst to know and to let my soul be watered by a way of viewing it that could offer fresh sustenance.

Recently a friend was explaining her process of adjusting to an unwelcomed change in her life that she was truly unable to effect. By becoming aware of her current belief system ("This shouldn't be happening, it's wrong, I don't like it") and then deciding to trust that it was all ultimately for the best, she set her intention to work *with* rather than *against* what was happening. Perhaps not surprisingly, not only did she come to perceive her own situation in an ultimately much more freeing way, but once she had, the situation also rather miraculously changed of its own accord toward an outcome she would have preferred at the outset.

Daunting, isn't it? That our whole world can change with a perceptual paradigm shift? Could I adjust to the ongoing unwelcomed change of a lost relationship with the desert and the disappearance of my deep friendship with it? I would like to stop hanging on to the insistence that any of the places on earth that I've loved always need to keep offering soulful respite.

When is it time to just let something be what it is? Can I lose my rigid insistence that something must be wrong for this unwelcomed change to have happened? Perhaps I could gracefully flex into another posture and work with, rather than against, "what is." After all, what has all that yoga been for, anyway? I breathe deep and can feel my ribs settling into an alignment I didn't realize they needed.

Perception, I am discovering, is everything. Recently, I attended a wedding full of fundamental Christians. Because I used to be one, I understood the vehemence with which they held their beliefs, but the harsh judgment I had received upon parting company with such believers years ago had been immense. In truth, I had projected both my need for and fear of a patriarchal system onto Christianity, yet even after leaving the church, was still afraid of being judged. Much to my chagrin, over time I came to realize that it was not so much about their judgment, or even God's, but how I was judging myself. My budding perceptions of a god I'd prefer to know had not yet caught up with my child self. Holding on to fear of a male daddy-god sending me to hell was my choice.

The wedding was a marvelous opportunity to see how far I'd come over the last thirty years. While there, I simply dropped into my heart and felt love for every person in attendance. After all, love is the center of any loving religion, isn't it? I suspected that the pastor, who just happened to come sit at my table during the after-ceremony dinner, sussed me out and decided I was one of the lost, who fortunately he saw no need to "save." But even if he had tried, I could honestly have gently told him, "Thank you for caring; Jesus already did that for me," and not worried about his judgment of a wine-drinking, independent, wild woman who howls at the moon and also delights in Goddess energies. At the outdoor wedding ceremony itself, I also noticed I had dropped cynical thoughts, like, "Oh, honeys, you have no idea what you're in for." Instead, I just sat in peace, even joy, entering into their happiness with them. The perfect summer afternoon weather was in complete alignment with my inner state. Shining. Elemental. Content.

But it seems that throughout our lives, opportunities to see and dissolve resistance (another way of shifting perception) abound. So now, in the midst of the desert, while reconstructing a new identity, I continue perceiving my need for extended quiet. Ironically, that is now being challenged by the sudden arrival of huge road-building equipment that has recently begun to chew and spit rocks all day long, right over the hill from my little sanctuary. The air shakes and the land quakes. I hear it as loudly indoors as I do outside. It makes me realize even more that I not only enjoy silence, I seem to absolutely *require* it to center and quiet my busy mind and sometimes angst-ridden soul.

Fortunately, this morning, because it is Sunday, the machines are not present, and the quiet of the mountain morning sun settles my mind into a profound reverie. All that punctuates the welcomed lack of noise is the twitter of various birds flitting past my porch.

Two bright red male cardinals appear: one on the branch of a Palo Verde tree and the other on a nearby boulder. After a brief stare-down between the two, one begins chasing the other from tree to tree. Perhaps the one being chased is an intruder, seeking to mate with an already spoken-for female. They are a gorgeous sight as they spread their astonishingly bright red wings and fly off up the canyon.

Now a large spotted brown Cactus wren flies to the ground right in front of me and then up to the tall, three-armed green cactus by my back porch, fluttering from place to place while investigating the gray scarred sections. Is he hoping to drill an opening for a nest? How does he land on the tops of those needled arms without hurting his feet? Oh, and here come two tiny hummingbirds. Every morning, at least one flies up to my face, noisily hovering within a few inches of me until he must decide I am not a food source or landing place. Wouldn't it be fun to think he's just saying *hello*? Always delighted with him, I grin, trying to hold still and not even blink.

I greedily take in this avian delight, because tomorrow, the respite of silence will likely be broken as the earth-gauging machines start up again. The birds will not come around. A small subdivision is being carved out in a small canyon 200 yards over and down the hill from me (thankfully, mostly out of sight) by huge yellow-necked reptilian machines that beep and crackle all day as they break up rock and plants to make a road. The land actually shakes. Every moment of such unwelcome noise has set me on edge. What happened to my serene retreat? *Beep. Beep. Beep.*

Perception.

Mine: I desperately need silence to repair my soul, to contemplate, to hear my teachings of how to live well because of the unwelcome disruption of loss.

Challenge: What if this external disruption is mirroring the inner?

Response: Oops. What if?

I ask myself if I can adjust to this unwanted noise by perceiving it differently. Maybe *it* is asking *me* to see this outer disturbance as a reflection of my current inner state.

I desperately want to figure this all out, but I have learned that overworking the mind leads to anxiety. I keep mistakenly trying to understand the heart's issues through my brain. As I recognize this, I drop awareness into my heart, and a small miracle begins to happen. I can physically feel myself slowing. My noisy, insistent mind starts to relax. Its cacophony begins to harmonize. My questions start to be tended to. Quietly.

I'm not sure of the exact relationship between mind and heart but I want to understand it better. Ha, there is the mind again. But mind is not the enemy. I want to be conscious. I want my heart to be the team leader and let it set the pace, working together with my mind, not so much like two excavating machines but more like a harmonious team of two horses pulling for the same cause. What cause am I intending? To cultivate a helpful perception of this loss of place. Who will the driver be? Me, of course. In my perception, God/life/opportunity has thrown down the gauntlet. How will I respond?

How can I trust that this loss of silence could be meaningful, even intentional to everything around it? I may be hitching up the team of mind and heart but it hasn't yet learned to pull together through this new phase. I see how much I resist the big noisy machines in the external world, preferring more natural, older, and quieter ways of moving earth. I understand the rippling of strong equine muscles to cultivate the soil more than the jarring angles of square machines that seem to be destroying it. I trust what seems more natural. Can I make peace with what *is*?

I am on the crux of understanding what surrender really is, learning to control less while still guiding my life and to feel my way along. But it is truly new territory. I am so close I can almost taste it. I see my team growing impatient, chomping at the bit. But still, not yet ready, I hold them back.

Trusting life and developing the ability to lean into instead of away from it is certainly culturally conditioned. At a young age I separated myself from the largess of life by absorbing several familial beliefs: *You are small and far from God. The heart is sentimental. The mind is everything but even it must submit to God. We have to do penance because we are sinners. If you fight God you will be struck down. You don't partner with God; you submit. Still, the mind is everything. The heart is a slight embarrassment. We don't create. Life is just as it is. You can pray but it's probably useless.*

But I am now weary and wary of those beliefs. As I age, I want to be more in my power, not less, intuiting that we are much more able to create than most of us realize. I have resisted claims that "we ARE God," preferring the co-creator stance, even if that keeps duality in place. It is simply more comfortable, at least right now. But if we are co-creators, do we actively set intention for what we are changing into, or simply trust that things will come up as necessary for our soulful evolution? Or both?

I assume that I need to have something that my environment is not providing (strength from Place itself), but should be. Guilt surfaces. Maybe I am asking the world to revolve around me. I hear my mother's exasperated, rasping voice, "Oh, you just think you're so entitled, don't you?" That would have been in response to some bright positive affirmation I might have said, such as, "I'm sure I'll get that house I bid on." Or even after a morning run: "I feel really great today!" I used to cringe at her sneering voice (who did I think I was to be so "up"?), so I would answer, "Everyone's entitled to the best life possible, aren't they? Isn't life meant to be good?" Sometimes she would slap me for that. She was fundamentally negative, so perhaps I felt I had to see the glass more than half full all the time to balance her darkness. *Or perhaps to protect me from my own.*

Darkness looms. Maybe I should release the perceived need for silence and "just get over it" (like she told me when she heard me lamenting after I found out I could never have birth children). Perhaps silence within became my refuge then and more important to engage with than the outer. Maybe when I've made my peace with this current loss, my outer world will be quieter, too. Or maybe I need to leave my monastic existence and just get out into the world and do more good for more people (to counter my mother's hissing, "Don't you just think you're so special"). I cringe, still expecting to be hit. She lost my trust when I was so young. So now I have trouble trusting God, having made him in her image. I didn't ever really want her anymore, either from any of her attempted kindnesses, but especially not from any of her criticisms.

With that, I suddenly realize that the children I parented for awhile didn't really want me, either. I am momentarily stunned.

A relieving thought trots in, however: their not wanting me was most likely, god willing, not my fault. As other adults in their lives discovered, they had been too damaged to allow anyone to truly parent them. My frustration and keen disappointment at that fact was perhaps not helpful, but my heart was always opening to them, in spite of my less-than-perfect reactions to some of their bizarre behaviors. I have had to learn self-forgiveness and also to forgive their birth parents and the god I imagined allowed their early damage, which in turn caused so much heartache for everyone. To do so and then let go. Events create perceptions, guiding actions, and results.

To adjust back into the present, I take a few deep breaths and once again release deeply embedded memories. Many years have now passed. I have learned that although silence can usher you into darkness, once you step into it, it will eventually bring you into light. Silence has become a constant friend and teacher. It creates space to hear how Spirit explains, forgives, and renews. It opens up space to realize the bounty of perceptions from which I have the freedom to choose. I can perceive myself as the embodiment of God or a co-creator, or both. Or neither. I can perceive the world as a blessing or a curse. Or both. I can perceive others or myself as powerful or weak. Perceptions form entire paradigms, building conscious or unconscious communities, cities, cultures, and worlds. If I am aware of how I have built and now live in the paradigms I've either bought into or created, I am free to enhance, discard, or change any aspect of the parameters.

How daunting! How freeing!

But challenges arise as long as we're alive. Perceptions can be so deeply embedded and intertwined with our past, upbringing, and conclusions we formed long ago that they may take some excavating to come to light. Maybe I can borrow that mean yellow machine over the hill to further uncover my own. Maybe I am doing that now, allowing the clamor and rumbling and tearing action to dig into my own old perceptions. *Beep. Beep. Beep.* If I keep letting my own earth rumble with self-examination and keep excavating the doors of perception, I might be able to clear the way for a freer outcome. Darkness to light. If I do, I am sure that new and more enlightening results will form. I think it will be beautiful.

And then I'll be ready to hitch up my lovely waiting team of eager horses pulling heart and mind together, plowing the field for increased life and love, cultivating more and more delight with which to live.

Today, may I open to the crumbling of a long-held perception of the necessity of outer silence as the precursor to a new paradigm that will lead to ultimate peace. May I utilize acceptance of "what is" as a template for increasing awareness of all perceptions that arise in love's gaze. When surrender is called for, may I see it as giving over rather than giving in. And when the road for building a new way to heal my heart appears, may I hitch up my team to attend to the task, eagerly striding into the welcomed unknown.

YOUR INVITATION

1. What one perception has most held you back?

2. How would you like to change it?

3. Are personal perceptions related to global ones? How so, or how not?

MONTHS 2-3

Chapter 10

I Get It (I'm Home and the Lights are ON)

It's hard to believe that I've now been in a state of strange dissolution for an entire month. Although I am looking and feeling more like a regular person (is that a good thing?), I still move in and out of a rather altered and contemplative state on a daily basis.

The epiphany I have recently experienced about needing outer silence because the inner has been so noisy has now settled into my bones. In the past week, even as the outer noise has continued, the inner clamor has sorted itself out, almost the way children do after tugging at your pants leg until you finally lean down and ask, "What *is* it?" Then they tell you, and it all begins to make sense.

If the old esoteric New Age maxim of "as within, so without" is correct, then my inner demand for outer silence was clearly overrun by the ruckus of my inner excavations. This has been big for me. This incessant construction noise seems to have served as a mirror of what has been going on in my inner world. It has been helpful to perceive it that way as a means of working *with* rather than *against* the noise. I have begun to release my judgments about the external horrors of raping and pillaging the neighboring land (after all, the land my condo sits on went through the same thing) and instead feel into that territory within myself.

From the inner rubble, many issues have begun to sort themselves out almost effortlessly and become clear. How an abusive mother pillaged my soulful innocence. How she did so out of her own disappointments. How she was human, just like me, just like you, only with perhaps more venom than some. And less than others! How moving to accept the outer as a potential gift rather than resisting it, and allowing my Inner Teacher to deliver helpful lessons just might craft a much more peaceful process and outcome.

As the morning sun once again parades across the canyon and seems to match my own sense of dawning relief, I am now freer to wonder what you, the one to whom I am actually writing all of this, conceive as your own relationship between your external environment and your internal self. I'm wondering what you have either learned so far through your own crucible of life experience or you suspect might still be waiting for you.

I'd like to share a process that has helped me. You can set a clearly worded brief intention to discover helpful information, thoughts, and feelings to support a past or current change you'd like to make peace with or a future change you suspect may be on its way, both on the inner and outer levels. What might that be? Take a few moments, if you're willing, to drop into your deep self and see, hear, or sense what change in some aspect of your life is asking for.

Pre-Meditation:

Word your desire (and write it down for future reference) in the positive, creating a sense of what it is you want, not referring to what you don't want. It could be something like, "I intend to discover what has been holding me back from…." or "I open to change in the area of…with grace and ease." Words expressing your own strongest values may be important to include, such as *love, trust, freedom, peace, grace, ease,* etc. You might want to say, "I want to trust my highest good is always unfolding with…" or, more specifically, "I intend to find a new job that inspires me and completely suits my skills and preferences." Or, "I want to look forward to finding a new partner." The idea is to stay in sentient desire, meaning that you are desiring a positive experience. The Law of Attraction will give you whatever you put out there, but since I'm assuming you are basically a good and kind soul, you will want to be attracting an elevating, not a de-escalating, process and outcome.

You may soar in this upcoming meditation, or you may instead need to enter into it several times before you discover your most potent experience. After an initial read-through of the following prompts, you might want to record it all in your own voice. We tend to believe our own voices the most thoroughly! You may also want to play some of your favorite soothing, wordless music in the background. Music is a magical transporter to other realms, helping us to travel out and back.

Meditation:

Let no one disturb you. Close all doors, turn phones off.
Use a timer with a soft bell, if needed,
set for around twenty minutes.

To begin, can you invite yourself to take a few breaths of any depth, wiggling into stillness without and within even if you're reading? If you are choosing to not record this in your own voice, can you instead allow your mind to process these words while you read them, paying the most attention to your own experience in the moment?

All right. Inform your mind that it will only be a short time until it can return to its normal functioning, and that, meanwhile, it might really enjoy relaxing and either observing or participating in this experience as it chooses. Letting your body wiggle a bit as it settles in, let yourself begin to relax, dropping your shoulders, taking a deep breath, beginning to let everything else around you fade... Notice how good it feels ... Let your eyes lose their focus as you go within, closing or remaining open as they wish. Take a few more comfortable breaths and, allow your already-chosen intention to arise effortlessly. What you want to...do...have...or be...what is it you want to release... attract... or experience in the next several moments... Take as much time as you need...

Let that intention crystallize again in your mind.

Notice how easy it is becoming to know that only the highest good supported by divine protection is what you will experience. This lovely experience becomes you ... Feel how deeply all your muscles are already relaxing ... letting go, letting go... easy, easy...

Softly speak out your intention a few times. Let it echo within.

Go very, very slowly now, the way a caterpillar crawls along a green leaf... and now you float free of that leaf and perhaps free of any body at all, on into the vastness of space. If you like, you can see or feel a gold cord securely flowing from your body to your spirit as you travel. You are at ease in your spirit, whether you sense it deep in your body or float beyond your physical being. You sense your true home; you are at ease in deep silence, where everything is possible but nothing has yet manifested. Outside noises fade to the edges of your experience whenever they arise.

Breathing more... allowing... receiving... being aware...

You breathe even more deeply now.... releasing, with relief, your sense of who you are in the world for the pleasure of merging with the safety and love of the Great All. You allow yourself to travel into a sense of the invisible world surrounding you.

*Notice if gratitude for creation swells up as you feel yourself
in the heavenly Field of All Possibilities, where everything
began and anything is always and forever possible...*

*You let yourself simply absorb and dwell in the vast
kindness of divine presence. You take a long time
here, where everything becomes timeless and you
are wholly absorbed in the pleasant moment...*

*Breathing deeply... Notice how easy it is to feel yourself
comfortably going deeper and deeper into your heart with each
breath ... Into your wise and loving self. Enjoy deep, even, rhythmic
breathing, until the breath becomes you... and you become it...*

*Notice how a sense of a loving presence is growing within and
all around you ... Feel how your readiness to meet something or
someone helpful is rising up out of the nothingness.*

Your heart recalls your intention.

*You begin to have words or just a feel for them, an impression ...
Your mind briefly contributes the words and then dissolves into the
intention itself, linking with your heart-space ...*

You begin to notice something forming within.

*It has a welcomed emotional feeling to it. You open even wider
to merge with the goodness it is offering. It might be a sense of love,
excitement, eagerness, relief, freedom, or deep calm. You gladly
recognize and embrace its offerings.*

*A figure or sense of a person or spirit being may be emerging...
Or an object you may or may not recognize. If you feel hesitant, ask if
it is there for your highest good. If it isn't, release it on an outbreath
and return to the vast kindness of space, allowing that which is in
your highest interest to manifest ...*

When all that is clearly there for your highest good is on the scene, you notice how easily these next moments unfold. Listen.... ask.... observe.... feel.... and receive. Whether a scene or story appears or not, you take great pleasure in a felt sense with whatever is present, absorbing sentience, new confidence, and wellbeing.

Ask your heart and mind to be in one accord with what is happening .... Let them inform you together as to what item in your life wants support for change, what wants to be excavated, carved out, or created anew in order to manifest your intention.... Notice how you have both the support of earth to stand upon and sky to be inspired by.... and how beautifully you are living between heaven and earth....

Taking plenty of time, feel into the power and beauty of that which has been excavated to make room for that which wants to be activated in you...

Without thought, let yourself know the
truth.... breathe it in.... in and out...
And with thought, let the mind inform you of its truth...

Just be with that which is unfolding in
kindness and compassion.

And now, when you feel it is sufficient, let the breath bring you back to this space and time. Slowly allow your eyes to open and re-focus. Take a few moments to consider your experience. Notice how both body and mind feel. Stretch, drink water, look around, at some point perhaps jotting down any notes you want to. Know that you are still integrating your experience into your body in this very moment.

....

Post-Meditation:

Were you able to concentrate or did your mind wander? Either way, what does your experience tell you? If you sank deep into meditation, what most impressed you?

What will you do with the information you gleaned?

We have so many ways of knowing ourselves. Whatever happens, even if an intentionally-focused meditation yields surprise, it is as helpful as we allow it to be. We can let it inform our outlook, reveal priorities, and provide direction. We have only to listen.

My own experience of this meditation, which I recorded beforehand, took me in a direction I felt guilty about (notice a cultural pattern there?) but was nevertheless a strong message. Not coloring within the lines or following the "directions" the meditation offered, I instead actually thought the whole time about the house I'd like to build in Hawaii. It would be a massive change from the small home I live in right now. It is a familiar dream that, if I sold my desert condo, or simply manifested more resources, or somehow just allowed and believed, could come true. It completely engaged my heart and soul. Though other beings did not come to me, as they have many times in the past, it was apparently not where my attention was focused. *Energy flows where attention goes.*

Though I did not find my way directly through my original intention, which was, "Help me work through the meaning of all this overload of thoughts about my entire life and shock at not connecting with the desert anymore," in a way, over time, and in retrospect, it did just that. It freed me from the recent past and brought me to an exciting possibility of truly making Hawaii my winter home. It was full of the qualities I'd realized were so alive and valuable to me: freedom, peace, joy, grace, and ease.

So, I let myself have that, trying not to judge anything and just accepting. When the peace and compassion of Hawaiian "aloha" seeps into my consciousness, and when I can luxuriate in it for a while, I find serenity rolling through my mind, body, and spirit. If I can let all of this current loss of relationship to the Sonoran Desert just be what it is, and keep gravitating toward peace, I will be fine. I will not ignore the big questions waiting for me out there; perhaps they are being answered right now in ways in which I'm not even yet quite aware, but will float into my consciousness soon. I will trust that, and myself. So, I don't have to have all the answers to feel at home and realize that the lights are "on." They're *on*! I don't have to know everything as a defense against a god I'm having trouble trusting. That issue has just faded with the shadows of a new day dawning. Just as some cancers are found to appear and magically disappear on their own, the cancer of the worried mind can and often does the same. We must remember how magical we really are!

How about you? Where are your own points of similarity and difference to my experience? What does that tell you? I wonder how you might be feeling about the content of your outer vs. inner landscape, the meditation that was offered, and your insights. I hope you are gathering substantial encouragement and increasing peace as you traverse your own inner terrain, regardless of what is happening in the outer. Sometimes the outer matches the inner, and other times it doesn't. You can make meaning of it either way. As we realized in the previous chapter, it really is all a matter of perception. We find our home when we settle with sentient paradigms, allowing compassion to guide us through change. And the vibrancy of love itself turns the lights ON.

Ancestors, God, Goddesses, Grandmothers
and Grandfathers, Angels, and
all beings who love us:

May You open our minds and hearts to the power of Your
presence in both our inner and outer landscapes.

*May we keep learning to surrender to a trustable
god as we encounter each new challenge.*

*And may all of us find that we are, through it all,
held safely in the arms of love.*

YOUR INVITATION:

1. What did your meditation reveal?

2. How do you know when YOU are "at home and the lights
    are ON"?

3. What do you appreciate most about the "inner journey" you're on?

Chapter 11

Life Magnifies Your Fears

Just when I began to think I was getting a handle on my journey, another challenge struck, an after-shock from the unplanned loss of soulful connection to the desert. I had just begun adjusting to my various spiritual losses, happily connecting again with other humans. One night during a lovely outdoor dinner with a friend, we were admiring a huge Saguaro cactus planted close to our table. It was massive and healthy-looking, tall and sure. As we were admiring it, I suddenly began seeing pulsating bright lights along the cactus flickering at the edges of both eyes and, eventually, floating black spots moving as my eyes scoped across the entire patio. Although the bright lights only lasted for a few moments, I went into immediate emotional shock. I told God I refused to have one more physical challenge than what I'd already been dealing with for the past five years.

For the next week, I tried to ignore it. Maybe it was bad tequila, or the fish. Then it happened again, this time upon waking two days later. An ill-advised choice to Google the symptoms on the Internet sent me into full-out fear and worst-case scenarios. I might be losing my eyesight! I felt frightened, alone, abandoned, irritable, and existential. Living alone, all was magnified. I didn't want to have to navigate a medical emergency all by myself. I also knew I would not want to live if I lost my vision. I immediately began working on healing myself by claiming health through thought and feeling (as taught by neurobiologist explorer Dr. Joe Dispenza) and called on all my angels, ancestors, and spiritual beings I'd ever known. My blood pressure was rising even as I was alternately claiming health and then trying to ignore the whole issue.

But because this vision "problem" could be irreparable if ignored (as some sites somberly warned), I made an appointment with an ophthalmologist. "Trust in God but tie up your camels" was a spiritual and practical mantra I had often used when I felt that a double-edged approach might be best. So I reminded myself to trust in God, continuing claims of perfect health, while tying up my camels by going to the doctor. My dinner friend's son, who has a nursing degree, very kindly met me there out of the goodness of his heart as an educated second set of ears for whatever the prognosis might be. During some of the more uncomfortable procedures for which neither the doctor or his nurse had any empathy, he also squeezed my hand and reminded me to breathe. Several nerve-wracking, painful tests later, the doctor announced that it was only a benign symptom of aging. If it got worse, he said, it would be obvious. Otherwise, there was nothing that I needed to do. Those flashing lights were not even an indicator that anything worse could happen.

Right there in the doctor's office, I developed a cold. I suspected that my fear had taken too much energy out of my immune system, and some of those little germs that are supposedly always surrounding us were invited into the stress party I had thrown for my body.

Appointment over, I thanked my friend's son and drove back home, coughing and feverish, feeling a mix of relief, chagrin, and puzzlement. What had all that fear been about?

"Much ado about nothing," I muttered to myself. How had I gotten my panties in such a wad (a graphic saying from one of my more earthly Breathwork teachers)?

The shock has taken a few days to subside.

I hear my mother's demeaning voice. "Who do you think you are that you shouldn't suffer? You think you're entitled?" *Entitled.* There it is again. It grates on the tender wound of my fear, scarring my faith. I look for the right attitude: a gentle entrance into perfect health, not a demand to a withholding god. I remind myself to breathe. (Even as I recall my mother's lack of kindness, I rush to remind myself that my father was lovely. A kind and caring man, he saved me from becoming a complete basket case, but was not able to prevent my mother's unwanted attentions when he was at work, which is when the worst things happened: some physical harm, but mostly emotional injury.)

And now, in the aftermath of the vision scare, I am left to wonder, "How much of this fear was related to my sense of never knowing a safe and trustable mother love? Is that related to feeling at the mercy of a dangerous god? How could I be more empowered in the future? What is my fear and distrust of Western Medicine about? Is it justified? If it is, then why don't I just avoid that route entirely? And why do I get sick at all? I know better!"

For all my professed self-assurance that we have the ability to heal ourselves through belief alone, sometimes I have very little faith in it completely working. And Western medical doctors seem so sure, so authoritative, so in control. But I cringe at the long tunnel I get sucked into if I let fear take me down the allopathic medical path without using my own discernment. I know there is a better way—a higher and more empowered one. Can I trust acting in alignment with my changing beliefs and increasing intuitions?

I have so much to learn. And such a long road in order to carve out trust in self and the type of god I want to know more intimately.

Gratefully back home from the sterile and jammed doctors' office, I am relieved to once again be ensconced on my sheltering back porch and gazing at the faithful Saguaro. I look at their brown scars, the nests built by birds who have found access into them for raising their young, and the older Saguaro whose graying ribs stretching along their arms are beginning to show. Some are dying and beautiful. When they collapse and fall over, they will provide shelter for certain desert animals who for some reason can only nest in their decaying forms. Yet they are still in their community. Whatever their age, all Saguaros tend to group together in colonies, large gatherings that roam easily up the canyons and hillsides. It seems significant that I realize they stop growing at a certain elevation because they instinctively know they couldn't survive the cold.

And then I understand the teaching. It becomes a prayer I give to myself: *May I also know where to grow myself, how to self-nurture for optimum growth, and how to recognize my own colonies all around me. Then when it is my turn, may my own graying and my own death be as beautiful as theirs.*

Ancestors, help me find my way through fear of physical illness so I don't panic again like that. May I learn what trust means as well as who and what to trust. May I know my own limits, thriving at the right elevation to support my own vibrant health. And meanwhile, may I offer a home for wildlife and wild life in the caverns of my own beautiful and scarred, still-living heart.

YOUR INVITATION

1. What concerns or even scares you most about your own physical health?

2. What stance do you take between trusting in God but also tying up your camels?

3. How do you live your best life regarding your physical present and future?

Chapter 12

The Gift of Your Natural Rhythm

It is mid-afternoon, and I am watching a sky-blue slow-motion day progressing along my back porch. Morning meditations transpired hours ago, and after other activities around the complex and errands in town, I find myself drawn once again to my outdoor desert sanctuary. I am recovering from my loss of this place as I once knew it, starting to appreciate life just as it is, remembering that I do still love and value the natural world in all its forms. It has actually been a perfect day, full of easy movement from one task or activity to another.

Days play themselves out best when I am able to let the hours unfold naturally rather than by forcing a prescribed tempo. Being retired now, I have that luxury. But how many of us, even in retirement, really allow ourselves to enjoy that gift? In Western culture especially, it is so easy to keep unconscious habits of a relentless pushing and rushing pace simply out of familiarity. All hard workers go to heaven, right?

Today I have been more aware of each moment, from event to event, asking myself, "What is best to do right now? Where is my energy, and what activity does it suit?" Whether the response is making phone calls, sitting down for a bit, tending to bills, or writing, I do that. I can almost hear a melody as I move effortlessly from task to task (or pleasure to pleasure, depending on my mood and any requisite responsibilities). I am sorry I did not develop more of this attitude throughout my work life. If I had, I imagine life would have been even easier than I thought it was at the time. Because I was self-employed and made my own schedule, I thought I had freedom. And to a certain extent, I did. But I still did not escape the automated rush from one activity to another, be it client appointment times, billing, gathering credits for licensure, planning and offering workshops, tending to godchildren, or even meeting with friends.

Of course, if I was partnered again, had a full-time job, children to raise, or others to attend to, my time would be completely taken up. But even then, I am sure that I would enjoy so much more ease if I would only tune into that universal hum playing right beneath my conscious mind. We all have that slow hum; it is just a matter of realizing and listening to it. You probably know it, too, even in your own busy life. That way, when you have to take your 10-year old to the doctor or make cupcakes for a school festival at the last minute, re-schedule a business meeting or attend a mandatory event, you can still accomplish it all with greater peace than imagined as long as consciousness leads from moment to moment. Your mind may think it has to do things a certain way, but your body might feel tension in doing so. There is one of your clues! You can follow your instinct while still satisfying your mind telling you everything that has to get done, only in a rhythm that makes you feel lighter, more aligned, and at peace. When your partner or colleague needs a listening ear or help with a task, you can acquiesce as long as you know that the hum is still playing just below the surface. But if it's not, maybe that is the clue for drawing a line. None of us need to be everything for everyone all the time. Selflessness is beautiful but martyrdom pinches off life force. It never lines up with one's natural rhythm.

You can access the rhythm of your own hum in many ways. If you've had a musical background, or even just enjoy listening to music, you can appreciate feeling of rhythm in your body, mind, and heart. You can link that feeling to how your body wants to move, even when doing menial tasks, how your intuition leads you to an order of "go," towards what brings your spirit alive, and by being in such awareness, how much energy you conserve rather than expend. Paying attention, you can fine-tune your ear and body to rhythm in general: the rhythm of a family, the rhythm of the earth, the rhythms of the day…

When I get too didactic and intense about certain subjects (like writing and revising), I can fall out of sync with the rest of my life (not exercising or eating well). I just don't move enough. I am most in sync when I make variety a priority in my day, including all the healthy choices I know will leave me satisfied at the end of the day. But when I don't, I am learning to ease up. I sigh, try not to judge myself, and just let my body make more of the choices than my mind the next time. It's amazing how wise the body is when we let it take front and center!

When I ignore my instinctive self too long, I feel no rhythm and have no satisfaction in the passing of a day, perhaps even feeling adrift and dampened. When I judge myself for this ennui, it seems to last longer. But when I practice self-compassion, it seems to pass sooner. My silent prayer to the universe is, "Let me gather the seeds from this now-unhappy state and blow the chaff away." If I can discover what I might be depressed about, I can then explore the antidote. But if I can't take it apart, I loosen my mind (I don't let it run the show), sit with the feelings or general malaise, hold it up to Spirit, spend time in nature, cry, grieve, and allow any old wounds to surface (even the ones I thought were long-since healed). Eventually, the sorrow abates and I am able to look around with eyes present to the moment. The morning dawns, the birds hop around, and I smile. I'm back to life as it is. A natural rhythm then ensues; I once again immerse in the flow. I might even recognize any angst I have so recently rolled through as part of that flow, the bend in the river where the water gathered energy as it collided with a large boulder mid-stream. With a chagrined laugh, I remember that water always finds its way around blockages.

How do you recognize your own rhythmic signature, no matter how much the melody changes? How do you cope with your feelings? If you repress emotions, you may think you don't have any. But that could be a recipe for all kinds of illness. So can constantly venting, however. I believe we each have an original, healthy, musical style in our emotional bodies that fluctuates over time and with age and life events; the trick is to hear the changing song of health and feel the rhythm of your own life. When you turn your attention to the subtle feeling in your body, the way blood is flowing through your veins, how it affects your heartbeat, how it plays throughout you like a finely tuned instrument, you'll begin to notice it even more. When you do, you'll breathe deeper, find yourself living in the present with greater ease, and realize the unique pace of the constantly changing energy that is you.

I love to tune into my own rhythms. When I do, there is always wisdom either encouraging me to stay with what I'm doing, to take a break, or to switch gears completely. Even if we have tasks at work or home requiring our immediate attention, we have so much more freedom in which to accomplish them than we realize when we let ourselves hear and feel that rhythmic hum inside. When we set our intention for whatever job we have to accomplish, we can still learn to trust our own internal rhythms to guide us in completing the task with a kind of vibrancy previously unknown.

Right now, my own humming buzz is changing. I think I've written enough, so before the sun sets I'm going to amble out along the trail leading down into the canyon. I'm changing gears. How about you?

May I hear and recognize my own unique, signature song that takes me through the rhythm of my days. May this comfort and sustain me, keeping me attuned to and aligned with the Universe.

YOUR INVITATION

1. How do you notice your own rhythms?

2. When do you realize you've ignored them and how do you then respond?

3. Where (what locations, under what circumstance, or with which people) are you most at ease with your own rhythms?

Chapter 13

Conscious Aging

For the past year, I have been trying to manifest a small local group that would be willing to focus on the process (and outcome) of aging. All I want is a place I can say my truth in a compassionate and mature setting and be deeply listened to, maybe even understood. No correction or advice. I just haven't been able to engage any of my friends to do so. I even queried some therapists and put up posters around town advertising a group ready to form. No response.

Why was that? I suppose the reasons were varied: busy lives, fear of dealing with aging head-on (I notice my judgment there), or just lack of interest. Finally, I asked a friend I'd not approached before about it. Sure enough, she had actually been "certified" to teach Conscious Aging classes, listing several authors who were exclusively writing about it.

Where have I been? I know so many consciousness teachers and authors, but hadn't seen any of that work or been to conferences dealing with it. But, oddly, I found myself recoiling to learn that this was already a whole spiritually developed study. With their apparently defined parameters, I could feel my own untamed borders about aging shrinking (wrinkling, really) and becoming uncomfortably squashed, reduced to fit a now possibly too defined topic. How could we ever truly tame either the process of aging or our own wild last moments, so filled with the unknown?

Before I began to draw as close to the divine as consistently as I do now, I was often conflicted about and afraid of aging. Afraid I'd feel I hadn't done all I came here to do or experience and, as a result, wouldn't be ready to depart. Afraid because I didn't want to have body parts break down. Angry that we have to die at all (and I am still not sure we need to). I didn't (and still don't) want pain or suffering or limitation. Who does? Or hospital stays, retirement homes, gray hair, or wrinkles. I am, unfortunately, still too inundated with our glossy-magazine body standards (which I will never live up to) and use those impossible criterions to self-judge. Most days, I am absolutely sure there is a way to experience self-acceptance and consistent good health without stress and duress. But I have other moments where fear rolls in and I feel a vague sense of panic, disbelief, and anger that we age at all.

However, some of those fears are dissolving as I explore them, even without a group with which to process. I do pray I will be healthy right to the end and just "drop my robes" (as Native people say) when the time is right. No muss, no fuss. I feel a growing power of alignment with what I call "Spirit," so connected with magic and miracles that I increasingly believe I have the power to effect a positive outcome. I don't begin to know the reasons for trying deaths that others experience; I can only speak of my own ever-changing awareness and intention of ease as I anticipate crossing over. That said, even with my Near-Death Experience I went through at age 27 (you can read about this in many of my other books), at times I still fight the very idea of death. Though the NDE taught me more about the power of surrender, the amazement of heaven, and the undiluted joy of being "on the other side," the challenges inherent in living here on earth have perhaps dulled the vibrancy of that knowing. So, actually, I find that I proceed as perhaps do most people who have *not* had an NDE: with confidence at times and not at others as I draw closer to the inevitable on the other side of the unknown.

Meanwhile, I feel best when I act on beliefs that help maximize my own personal power to thrive. That is why I am so attracted to the work of quantum physics neuroscience consciousness explorers, such as Dr. Joe Dispenza, Gregg Braden, and Dr. Bruce Lipton. I appreciate that, through fascinating research, they have developed a matrix of teachings on how to manifest our natural state of health by setting intention and fully feeling the emotion that goes with those desires. Through epigenetics of the resulting cellular signaling, we teach the body to live the chosen future outcome as though it was already happening in the present.

For example, if you want mobile joints, you frequently practice *feeling* delight in healthy joints before they actually feel better. If you want to be pain-free, you *feel* the exhilaration of that ease. You teach your cells a new state, of ease and wellbeing.

Marvelous.

The deepest part of my belief system has told me for years that there is no reason to have pain *or* the attendant suffering that infuses it; we all have the capacity to enjoy perfect health. It is actually similar to some religious teachings only without insisting on a prescribed perception of God. Though sometimes it seems like massive personal and cultural paradigm-busting work, as I age, I am increasingly motivated to regularly incorporate this healing approach. I am learning how to engage my true desires and live in highly satisfied emotional states in the present even before the results have appeared. It does take repetition, but it is a practice I love to do.

Reports of spontaneous healings around the globe happen often for those who may or may not subscribe to this particular cosmology. But in all healing, somewhere I think someone (human or angelic) is envisioning the healing. At any rate, I am teaching myself where and how I want to focus my own mind and heart, and, through practice, am slowly growing in awareness of how to better engage with and increase my own empowerment. Some of the results are actually miraculous.

Manifesting from the "field of all possibilities," as Quantum Physics describes and channeled "Abraham" teachings explore, suggest that aging of body and mind could be actually more about perception than a phenomenon over which we have no control. For some reason, I'm all in with this. I am increasingly on the path of manifesting the joy of living. The more I meditate, often with eyes open, taking in the world, the more joy I feel, the more synchronicities appear, and the more health, love, peace, and abundance I manifest. I particularly tend to focus on health as I age. In moments where my adult self thinks my body probably will actually die, I also realize I don't need to live a long time, as some in this consciousness work plan to; I just want a measure of completion and the peace I imagine will accompany that accomplishment. However, I must admit that at other times I don't think I'll age or die at all. That thought could either be denial or my exuberant inner five-year-old who never ages! I, of course, prefer to think the latter. I also wonder if perhaps she is actually connected with a far older and wiser self who knows, or remembers, our vast potential.

What are your own contradictory beliefs around aging? Can we gather these seeming contradictions into our hearts and relax with them? Might any resulting initial friction lead to an alchemy that burns the dross of opposites and leaves the gold of a unified awareness? Living beyond the opposites opens up new worlds of freedom.

Assuming my body will most likely die at some point, I still want to keep envisioning an easy and painless passing over. However, my own family members' deaths have left a legacy of terrible suffering before and during their passing. My stomach clenches when I remember their last months and days, even as I seek to allow those memories to fade away. I have no familial model for an easy death, so I suppose I'll once again feel as though I'll be pioneering the road less taken.

Actually, I've done this for much of my adult life anyway. In the 80s and 90s, I offered new experiential body-mind-spirit techniques that were incredibly powerful yet did not require belief in a specific God; as a result, I had Christian ministers calling and telling me I was Satan disguised as an angel of light. Though it quite hurt my feelings at the time, I now laugh, because I realize that the darkness they feared was not my own. And having moved into and then through fundamental Christianity for several years myself, I understood their fear. On into the 90s and up to my professional retirement in 2012, in my once-small and provincial Montana town, I offered a highly ethical form of Breathwork as a way to develop insight and effect personal healing, but even that was looked upon with suspicion by some fellow therapists! And then there was my own version of Sound Therapy: blowing various tones into parts of the client's energetic body, an entirely intuitive move on my part. Though now there are fully trained "Sound therapists," even in the early 90s, few seekers, even those on board with body-mind-spirit modalities, were open to receiving this seemingly unusual therapy. In the new millennium, I also created my own form of Voice Dialogue that was sometimes scary for the initiate but always rewarding for the courageous. I had to remind myself how long it took to get comfortable with so many alternative approaches myself. Those were poignant memories: intensive, loving workshops where, as both learners and participants, our own psyches and hearts at first resisted but eventually flew so wide open that we'd gladly receive all types of healing.

These marvelous life-enhancing workshops I've both attended and taught have helped me build a firm foundation through the tenants of Transpersonal Psychology, which acknowledges the importance of a sense of the divine and paranormal experience as actually being normal! It has enriched and stabilized me tremendously in the tenants of a loving God/Goddess/Universe for the ever-changing perceptions I keep cascading into and through. Each time I've gathered the courage to thoroughly explore my own depths, I discover something marvelous in my psyche and spirit, some old hurt that needs to be assuaged or some new perception waiting to bloom. The initial difficulty eventually yields a rainfall. I am like the thirsty desert Saguaro, expanding my ribs to receive moisture from Heaven. I've explored the inner terrain frequently, perhaps due not only to early wounding but also from all the therapy trainings I attended and the time I've had in living alone for so many years. All of it has helped poise me toward the death my body may someday experience (my inner child wanted me to state it that way).

No matter our age, we learn so much just from being alive, and can continue to taste the goodness of life with each passing year. Wisdom is the award-winning wine of experience, the distillation of flavorful passion and desirability (an adaptation from what I learned while touring the California Sonoma Valley vineyards). You can't rush results. You have to absorb the right amount of moisture and suitable temperatures to enjoy a great harvest. There are even vineyards in the desert. Who would think that grapes would flourish there? But with the right environment, and enough water, they do.

That is what we do, too. We flourish best by planting ourselves in the right place on earth that supports our sustenance. We water and fertilize ourselves with nourishing thoughts. We attract the right amount of sun by opening to love, light, and a vibrant spirituality, increasing our attention to it as we age. Some of us can even thrive in the aridity of the desert. I choose to flourish in all landscapes while allowing myself to linger in the ones that most support joy and wellbeing. Even as I age. Or perhaps because of it.

By the way, during the writing of this chapter, I actually manifested a group to deal with the topic of aging. We meet weekly now; it has been rich and all I hoped it would be. Go figure. Thank you, neuroscience!

May I deepen and dwell in the truth of my conviction that we are designed to be healthy throughout our lives. May I carefully attend to fears of aging or any manifested illness that seems so contrary to my beliefs. And may I crawl into the lap of the divine within and without to help me know whether to expect to morph illness into wellbeing or to somehow make peace if pain persists. I am a work in progress; I am fearlessly and wonderfully made.

YOUR INVITATION:

1. Has your belief system about pain, suffering, and aging changed over time? How so?

2. What is still conflicted in you about aging, or has it settled? How so?

3. What spiritual being(s) can you turn to for support, even advice?

Chapter 14

Who's in Control?

Three months into my life-changing descent, I awake shortly before dawn, as usual. I am aware of a new, strange relief to have not been in control of this initially unwelcomed change of relationship with the desert because it now feels like some kind of sacred event, and much larger than myself. In an odd way, it seems to have had control of me, or perhaps has transpired in conjunction with a deeper intention of which I had no glimmerings. Until now. Maybe it is also life being life, moving from chaos to order, and I am rolling along within its mystery.

At any rate, I am feeling privileged to have had so much time to let this experience have its way with me and to explore all the issues that have arisen, mostly unbidden, for my heart and mind to turn over and examine. As I stretch my limbs and wander out to what I now refer to as 'the outdoor office' on the back porch, I realize I'm feeling freer and breathing deeper than I have in several weeks. Much of it has to do with having had to surrender to forces beyond my control, daring to trust what I could not understand. Fighting change became futile; learning instead to crawl inside it to see what gifts might be available has offered many benefits, not the least of which is a newfound ease. I am judging myself less and listening more, pausing to ponder and seeking even greater surrender, suspecting that this seemingly chaotic process I've been rolling through could be carrying a template for collective and evolutionary change.

In the moment I consider this, it is as though the heavens in the sky above open up for a moment and a light even stronger than the sun bathes the landscape all around. It offers the animation of everything playing itself out in divine order, not just for me, but for all of us, whatever we're going through in our lives. My eyes widen and breath ceases though I'm still being oxygenated; something finer and wider is breathing *me*.

Suddenly I'm in another experience of the majesty of how Consciousness itself keeps either introducing us to new terrain or deepening us into the old. Or both at the same time! My body sinks into a vibrant yet relaxed peace. I am in awe of God, Creation, and the All That Is, within and without. Mind and heart are effortlessly aligned, as though my heart is thinking and my mind is feeling. I remain this way for quite awhile.

This experience of what Eastern cultures might label "Satori" eventually fades, however, as most of them seem to do. I am left speechless and without thought, just gazing out at the desert once again. I wish I could keep this impression forever, because I know that at times I will likely still squint up into the heavens as though sizing up 'the enemy,' much as a lizard does to look more impressive to his potential competitors. Other times I will release my demands to God, dancing with the wind, like the butterflies that flit by my outdoor seating. Yet now, after these past weeks of feeling so much angst and energy drained from my initial loss of connection, I have rested up and have fortunately begun to find my own rhythm through the labyrinth of self-discovery. I am still in the midst of change but now more comfortably walking the path by braille.

So much is happening in the outer world without any control or direction by me: birds gather, plants grow, seasons change, people suffer and die. On the inner, I am my own participant in both the sorrows and joys of the world. Yet I am still exploring what measure of control I have, how much I am not using, and who else might be running this change I'm still in the midst of. Something greater than my own volition seems now to be offering a benevolent design.

Or is it controlling instead? How much am I controlling with respect to the outcome and the origin of this paradigm challenge in which I've been so immersed? Who is the authority? What is true power, and how do I exert an appropriate amount of control with it? Is that possible? My mind has once again taken up the mantle of attempted control. However, I don't want to disrespect these thought processes. They are surely as important as how my heart feels. I just want the two to keep integrating.

Because I know I'll soon be leaving Tucson for a few months in the Hawaiian Islands, I do have a sense of urgency to understand more of what this leg of the journey has been about while still in this desert locale. When I become wary of a growing sense of newfound ease (which seems odd though agreeable to my insecure mind), I revert to questioning how much I actually run my personal life and how much I might be at the mercy of the vicissitudes of life or some god's control. I want to feel I can craft my present and future by being in alignment with my sense of the divine, but am I? I want to trust that decisions I've made are good and right for me, but are they? How much of my life is destiny, like a pre-ordained future, and who has pre-ordained it? Is it my destiny to control or is control that creates my destiny? I am again lost in a labyrinth, trying to feel my way through questions that actually seem crucial to the aftermath of this experience: questions that will craft how I will choose to live in the world as I go forward. I do want to allow my mind to be informed by heart and spirit, trusting that all three will relax best when working together. Like Father, Son, and Holy Ghost? Like Maiden, Mother, Crone? Like two lovers infused with the Beloved?

Perhaps the idea of control is really a myth, a fabricated reaction to a perceived lack. Perhaps it houses an existential fear that, underneath it all, no one and nothing else is in charge. An intriguing book by Intuitive Life Strategist Robert O'Hotto, *Transforming Fate into Destiny*, acknowledges that while certain fated variables are unchangeable (physical characteristics, gender, race, and maybe some major life trajectories), we still have many life choices where we can steer our ship while linking with Spirit to follow clues along the way. As I seek to work out my own philosophy, it seems that at the very least, we do indeed influence our destiny by our attitudes and choices. We can see or ignore, sabotage or enhance opportunity. Yet, in a different vein, the Abraham channelings by Esther Hicks pronounce that we are the total deciders of all we want and all we experience, the Law of Attraction at work. That seems to put us squarely in control. But even Abraham asks us, after specifying what we want, to not attempt to control the timing and even ultimate outcome; we are admonished to allow the Universe to fulfill our desires in its own time and way.

Are all of these systems various approaches to who has the reins? Are they belief systems, and as we follow them (whether doing so consciously or not) do we experience the resulting outcome of those paradigms? The paradigm of control I've probably been operating under is that 1) I have to do it all myself or it won't happen, and 2) I can hold danger at bay by steeling myself against a powerful God who surely isn't as trustable as I am to myself. It is tough to realize I have held these attitudes.

This is disturbing; for much of my life I really must have seen God as the enemy. It is such a contrast from my many declarations of the goodness of God, the Universe, and the many paranormal experiences I've had with Ancestors and Angels, let alone my incredibly inspiring Near-Death Experience. I would far prefer to morph into a cooperative stance with God. I love the idea of co-creation but don't know quite how to do that. I'm afraid I just keep repeating kindergarten, never graduating or truly progressing. What is truly controllable in one's life? And who is at the helm? Or if we are to dance together, both human and divine, how do we learn the steps? What will that look like and how does that feel? I have a growing suspicion that how we feel really does matter; it is probably our intuition trying to guide us. If we let it. If we trust it.

I let go for the moment into trust.

As I do so, the morning sun suddenly splashes light up the sloping mountain across the canyon from my little retreat. A deep sigh arises from my body. My body. The place that seems to have a life separate from my mind. The place where instincts rule and feelings reign, aligned with the power of the earth.

My body is connected with the natural world; nature itself does not seem to worry about any of this. The sun rises and sets, weather patterns and seasons come and go, and day follows night. All of it seems to run by instinct and cohesion; even chaos eventually morphs into some kind of order. Perhaps I am finally ready to allow my long-held need for control to change, willing to stand naked and undefended to see what helpful energies would like to live in me, ones that could help me discern when to either simply accept or take action for whatever is necessary.

But as soon as I say "naked," I start to shiver. I become afraid that if I really let go of perceived control, then abusive dark forces and negativity could take hold, the way my mother used to take hold of me. Oh…

It is hard to allow anything now in my adulthood that is not full of love and light. So if I let go and surrender, I become afraid. What if I really do let go? To what or whom? Will I get into an accident? Will that god destroy me? My inner child is hyperventilating. My protective inner masculine and feminine selves vehemently claim, "No one gets to override us anymore." My blood pressure is rising. I suddenly remember the fear prior to leaving my abusive upbringing.

"No more!" I had exclaimed to myself, when finally able to leave her household. "I will have nothing to do with anyone who is cruel or controlling or even slightly unkind."

Oh, now I'm at the center of the labyrinth. *I am seeking to be in control to conquer and be safe from the abusive parent who keeps trying to control me. It is she I am afraid of, not the kind god and goddess of my current understanding with whom I have perfect freedom to seek and have had so many benevolent experiences. My mother truly became the all-powerful, masculine, emasculating god of power in my small life. And it has taken me all this time, until just now, after she has already passed over and I am in late middle age, to fully realize it.*

I feel such a deep sorrow about this, even so sad for how frustrated and disappointed she must have felt throughout her own life. I have sought control to keep me safe from abuse! It is not related to the god/goddess/spirit that I have been choosing and coming to know at all!

Sometimes it gets very simple. We can operate through fear or love.

In that moment, I release and bless my mother where I imagine she now dwells in the heavens. I am amazed as I feel that she immediately begins to dwell redeemed in the heavens of my heart.

Forgiveness is full of surprises.

As I stand naked before this newer, kinder sense of spirit, it is still hard to know how much this power wants or needs to be in control of my life. Am I so separate from Him/Her/Creator? Does this power dwell primarily without, within, or both? Even while questioning, I begin to more comfortably sink into the questions while still holding them up with open palms and relaxed eyes. I breathe.

In the same moment, I finally feel the Ancestors, actually at the waterfall but calling to me from the mere mile that separates them from the back porch of my condo. They are simply nodding, and smiling, as it were, full of love and approval. The longest sigh escapes from my chest. I breathe them in. I am at peace. *I am sealed by the Light, by love and wellbeing.*

My last few moments on the porch this morning before preparing to leave for Hawaii are filled with relaxed and inspired thoughts. We all carry the essence of a greater spirit from which we originate and to whom we return. Maybe I AM that divinity housed in human garb come to experience joy and sorrow, peace and strife. And this Divinity we carry within helps us bridge to the other side beyond opposites! I go within body and spirit to find and develop my own wise counsel. Wings and roots. Oh, I like that. A long tube of healing vibrates right down through the center of my body. Separation dissolves. Unity arises. I am at one with everything. The morning sun and I now have much in common. We *are*, and it is good.

During my recent flummox of the awkward dance with God where I descended into a morass (Chapter 2: *"I'm A Mess"*), I was surely wrestling with my mistaken notion of how much control I really have. My illogical, child-driven, barely-conscious premise has probably been: *If I steel myself against anything I don't want, and stay in control, that will keep me safe.* How that would logically work, I don't know. It was an old belief of understandable origin in the midst of outliving its usefulness. But I am safe now. I might as well let my whole self know it. Really know it.

Perhaps feeling a need to control is always an understandable lack of faith in a benevolent power, whether internal or external. If we trusted our capacity to link with such a power either within and without, or both, we could use it for good. So many people in the world today are doing this already. It is time for me to get on board. I can bring along my flaws and imperfections. This journey is a "come as you are" event anyway. We bring our dreams and damage with us, morphing as we go, whether or not we or a divinity outside of us is directing it.

With this, thoughts thankfully fade. Even though it is still early morning, my eyes are growing heavy. It takes energy to move energy! The sun is moving up higher in the sky and I am still rocking on my lovely back porch. (You probably think I live here; in truth, I rather do.) I breathe deep, look up, and see that several birds have arrived, navigating newly accessible branches from the recent tree trimming and thinning I did. *The outer mirrors the inner?* A cactus wren gingerly hops and flaps up to the large Saguaro directly in front of me, the one with generous arms and enlarged ribs. He (she?) sits in the crook of all three arms (a possible future nesting site?), looks around, and flies off, quickly returning with long strands of brown grass. A chickadee hops along the ground ten feet in front of me. Perhaps he is looking for bits of grit or maybe succulent bugs who have burrowed deep in decaying twigs. Like me, he is just exploring, looking for nourishment. He will persist until he finds what he needs. Oh, now my round orange-bellied avian friend flies in and lands on the porch railing; he glances at me a few times, fluffing out the peach-colored fur on his little chest and releasing it, like taking a deep breath. Such is the quiet progression of morning (minus the incessant road-building noises in the background). Today the birds do not seem to mind it so much, and, in truth, neither do I. A wide love spreads across my body, soothing thoughts and muscles. I do not even question where it is coming from, or why. I just breathe.

So, in the coming days, as I prepare to leave the desert for the next three months to revel in the aloha of the Hawaiian Islands, I take both much and little with me. I am releasing imagined control over my desert experience and am morphing into an acceptance of everything just as it is. I see the desert with new eyes now: newly knowing, not expectant, aware. Aware to the moment, thoughts and heart aligning, the singing of the birds, the scuttling of squirrel, the rustling of dry grasses in the shortened winter days. With the sun, always the sun, illuminating all the dark places, giving them respite at night so they can rest and recover. As do I.

Even with such acceptance, I still cherish the vision that I've carried most of my adult life of us all realizing the sentient realities of a heaven on earth where nothing suffers or dies, nothing is predated upon, and every creature lives in comfort and joy. In that place, control of any kind is not needed because all is in perfect, agreed-upon harmony. In this moment, I release ideas about how and when and where that will happen, has already happened in another dimension, or is even happening now... *Ahhh....*

May I offer up the issue of control to a loving Creator
Who thrives within, without, or both!

May I link my spirit to Great Spirit to remember original intent.

May I fill my heart and mind with the
wonder of the best life possible.

And may any contradictions be embraced and
alchemized through the realities and power of love.

YOUR INVITATION:

1. What is your relationship to "control"?

2. When have you allowed a long-held personal paradigm to shift and what has been the outcome?

3. When are you most at peace with how the universe seems to work?

Chapter 15

Grace and Ease

The first thirty days after arriving in the desert passed like a fog; as I began to lighten up and adjust, thirty more also appeared and disappeared, time itself teasing me with a new-found ease. Now almost thirty *more* days have passed. Three months! I am still in the desert for a short while and have begun to find a pleasing rhythm to my days, although swimming in the outdoor pool is getting a bit chilly. Fall has ended and winter has taken over. At only 60 degrees by noon, and with blood thinned out by warmer desert days, I am actually shivering. I am still greeting each 40-degree morning on my back porch, which now feels like a benevolent witness to all I've been through. My toes, though, unprotected in flip-flops, are beginning to ache with cold.

The morning sunrise today was lovely, with bright patches of mountain-top sun, followed by pink skies turning light yellow, and on to that quick splash of light illuminating all the eastern edges of the stately Saguaros. But as the day has progressed, a strong gray overcast has moved in, keeping the sun from delivering her warming rays. So, I reluctantly leave my well-worn Mexican rocking chair on the back porch, retreating to the kitchen table, where the expansive north and west wall of windows afford their stunning view of the huge mountain range of the caverned and hummocky Catalina Mountains.

I'm still cold indoors. My Montana friends would laugh at my wimpyness. For them (and to me, before I started spending winters in warmer climates), a 60-degree day in winter is worthy of shorts and maybe even flip-flops. Well, I am in flip-flops, I'll have them know. I'm just cold in them. Environment changes and shapes us in many ways.

Though I have not recovered my former soul-connection with the desert, during these last three months I have begun to at least feel closer to the land. I spend considerable time feeling appreciative of it while winding through the small patch of desert I now call my backyard. I have cleared out enough sticker-laden bushes to enjoy easy walking and sitting in private enclaves on small and large pink and gray boulders. Sometimes I even dare remove my flip-flops and risk a sharp needle or two in order to once again feel the gritty, sandy soil under my feet.

Lately I've been talking to the land and the Ancestors, telling the desert that I do love it and am sorry for not being able to reach into it in the same ways I had for so many years. I'd love to experience that searing soulfulness again, so I ask the Ancestors to return that former passion if at all possible, if it is in the "grand plan." I simultaneously ask myself that question, referring to my own divine power. I'm still working out the "divine without/divine within" process, but now it is with an easy curiosity and a reference point within a more fully integrated heart-body. Meanwhile, I realize I am perhaps re-forming a relationship with the desert, much like human partners do who choose to stay in touch or perhaps actually together even when they have fallen out of love. This new relationship, probably like theirs, is quieter and more contemplative, gentler and more accepting. And I am moving through it with "grace and ease." Finally. Do estranged partners find ardent love again? Some do. Some don't. But grace and ease don't worry about it one way or the other. They just respond from their being.

I might have first heard the term "with Grace and Ease" (capitalizing them to endow these qualities as entities of sorts) from a trusted psychic, Leanne Doty, in Sun Valley, Idaho. Perhaps it was suggested by a wise long-time friend in Montana. All I know is that it came into my consciousness about two years ago and I immediately embraced it. It was the way I wanted to experience life and finally realized I could. I initially imbibed it whole-heartedly, but it has not yet become a fully traveled path in my consciousness. I keep straying off-road, probably because whenever memories of woundings arise, they carry the energy of Awkwardness and Discomfort, heading in the opposite direction of Grace and Ease! Those previously unconsciously held patterns of memories are often driven by their own nature of harsh insistence, incessant demands, and complete lack of light-heartedness or joy. I've either learned them from my culture, family, whatever soul issues I've needed to work out during this lifetime, or perhaps just by being a member of the human race. If we carry the capacity for all ways of being, both light and dark (which I consider likely), and if our souls have chosen a certain path of awareness (to mitigate rather than ignore the dark), then whatever the origin of the disturbance, I owe it to myself and all others to allow consciousness itself to teach me the very qualities with which it is effortlessly aligned: Grace and Ease.

Grace and Ease. Grace and Ease. I could breathe that litany in and out forever and take this inseparable pair to bed with me like lovers. Rise up with them. Watch the sunrise, go about my day, encounter challenges. With Grace and Ease. Who wouldn't want this dynamic duo in their entourage? The more I court these qualities, the more they acquiesce—the more I move into them, the more they become me.

This has been my gift. We all need these blessings if we are to live well. Grace and Ease have returned me to a state of wellbeing and trust, a quiet rhythm, and a hum that lilts through my days, even when trying circumstances arise. As a result, the outer environment has begun to effortlessly match this glorious feeling state pervading my waking and sleeping hours. It must be connected to the energy of the Divine Matrix that Gregg Braden so adeptly describes, the understanding that we are all connected as points in a web of light.

This morning, as the sun continues to spread its warming light across the family of Saguaros dotting Ventana Canyon, a six-inch long chipmunk darts out from under the brush and scampers up a small boulder (which I'm sure seems very large to him). Six inches long including his long tail, that is. He slaps his tail around several times as though announcing his presence. Or maybe he is boasting his territory. Or testing the air for predators, though his rapid movements seem more likely to attract rather than repel them. Watching me closely, he runs off his tall vantage point, and, to my surprise, skitters closer. I stop rocking and stay motionless. I must have passed his safety test because he finds a patch of shade on the ground right where my open back gate meets the sandy soil and, only three feet from me, drops to his belly with haunches splayed out behind him, tiny front arms spread-eagled as though he is about to ascend into the air. I want to laugh at his "flying ground squirrel" rendition and wonder if I should clap. A small chortle does escape my lips and he merely tilts his head toward me. As I continue to watch, his pint-sized head begins to bob downward and soon it is touching the ground. His eyes blink a few times and then close. He's taking a nap!

I feel ridiculously honored that this small creature would grace me (yes, Grace) with such trust. My own breath slows and I feel his surprising Ease in my own body. How long has it been since I have so consciously and completely let go in the presence of another? And how odd does that feel to have this experience with a chipmunk! His eyes remain closed. My own eyes feel heavy. Maybe I could take a small nap, too, but I don't want to miss a minute of his visit.

He stays resting that way for two to three minutes, taking slow little rhythmic breaths, while I tilt my head this way and that to appreciate him from different angles. Just when I think I might go ahead and nap, too, he opens his eyes, bolts upright, sits for a moment while assiduously cleaning his front paws, and, without a backward glance, races off, back into the underbrush.

Now I can freely laugh aloud. I think of the American Naturalist John Muir and how much I would have liked to share this simple moment with him, and how many other people there might be in the world right now who would love to share this moment, too. So I am, with you. My heart is full.

Now, several species of birds begin to streak by my corner of the desert, chirping and whirring and catching bugs mid-air. A beautiful full-bellied dark brown bird with tiny white spots flies next to my open porch gate and rummages around in the soil next to my feet, inches from where the chipmunk was just taking his nap. I hold very still except for the smile spreading across my face. Soon he, too, flits off, but he has affirmed the state of being I have so gratefully been feeling as I have been writing about to you this morning: Grace and Ease.

Life is a gift.

May we all find our equivalent of "Grace and Ease" moving forward, even through difficulty, with courage and wisdom.

May we live in as gentle a manner as possible, increasing in love every day.

And may we come around to the great privilege it has been, and is, to be alive on earth in the company of all other life forms dwelling here, too.

YOUR INVITATION:

1. What does "grace and ease" mean to you?

2. What qualities (values) do you most cherish?

3. What in general makes your life the most lovely?

 # MONTHS 4-6 

Chapter 16

Island Interlude

For the past few weeks before departing to the Hawaiian Islands, I've been increasing my actual meditation time on my little back porch in the desert. I've resumed listening to CDs like Deepak Chopra and Oprah's "Desire and Destiny" 21-day series and Quantum Physics-oriented morning meditations. I've been reading related books voraciously, absorbing goodness like the chipmunk who keeps returning to run over the tops of small boulders, nosing around to find food. Like him, I am scampering from place to place as I explore a deepening evolutionary inner landscape, and, like him, only choose that which nourishes.

This undisturbed retreat-like atmosphere has been perfect for the realizations I've been having. The lack of outer disturbance has allowed any remaining hidden inner disturbances to surface, be felt, seen, and thought about, to be turned over in the palms of my hands, wondered at, gentled, and either released or allowed to dissolve. I feel new, different, and much more at ease with the unknown specifically and with life in general. My pre-planned vacation in the islands arrives at the right time.

Except I am a bit apprehensive. I've just finished adjusting to the lack of my keen connection with the desert. What might I find in the islands whom I have also loved so well? Will that have changed, too? Fortunately, I am surrendered enough to just shrug my shoulders and remind myself that "what will be, will be," and go with it.

The moment I land in the Kailua-Kona airport, however, the relief is palpable. I look up to the lush green mountains, down to the frothy sea, and grin: "I'm home!" And so it is, for the next three months, with the embrace of Aloha—warm, unconditional love—from people and place, plants, and animals. I wander along my favorite beaches, rock in hammocks at sunset, drink a few too many Mai Tais, and even get a bit bored. Guilt arises. "Why aren't you doing more for other people?" I hear my mother's voice hiss. I question it myself. Should I be involved in rescue efforts of some kind, somewhere in the world? Have I become too selfish?

Each time I wonder, I take a deep breath and ask my divine self to help me know, be aware, and trust that I will respond in whatever manner I need to. I remind myself, as others have told me, that a simple, kind and loving energy extended to others is worth a great deal, maybe even every bit as important as some great accomplishment. I look up and pray that any resistance I have to just "being" will become assuaged by the aloha love that I know is so vast. Until I feel an actual prompt to take more specific action in the world, I continue to simply love and be loved by everything in the fragrant culture of Hawaii. Hawaiian friends comment on the fact that they love my smile and thank me for doing that, even though I've not been aware that I do.

I excitedly learn more native customs and language, receive and give hugs to Hawaiians and non-Hawaiians alike, and continue to smile, laugh, and contemplate. I meditate more than ever, with open eyes gazing at the ocean and closed eyes transporting me to the place beyond the senses. I kayak with whales who surround me, hearing their newborn babies' querulous questions and quips, listen to the mother's sonorous replies, and settle into the liquid power of the ocean's life. I kayak often, stroking in total contentment, the heart of the universe pulsing through both my own and everyone else's experience paddling by me on the ocean's surface. My body, mind, and spirit line up, and I move as one with the drift of days.

Today I choose pieces of loose beach coral and driftwood to construct a ceremonial miniature Medicine Wheel near the water, claiming my new life and my ability to create it. I speak out my aligned feelings and thoughts to the Universe while I pray, contemplate, and rest. My desert early morning rocking chair has been traded for a tattered lounge chair someone discarded on a private stretch of beach, and it suits me fine. As sunrise progresses, I watch tourists from the lovely Mauna Lani resort to my right playing in the water as to my left the catamaran snorkel-sailboat glides in and out of the quiet Makaiwa Bay harbor. Later I will snorkel, or kayak again, or just swim. I will dry off in the sun and seek shade under one of my favorite Banyan trees.

Weeks pass like days, and days like moments, and though I am recovering nicely from the shock of losing my desert lover, I now must also say goodbye to the islands and prepare to fly back for a last planned month at my now-historic Tucson condo before returning to my Montana home. I continue to feel different: consistently better, happier, and, somehow, new. Really new. Easily trusting life. Much more present to the moment and seldom derailed by the past. Even "good" past memories seldom surface. I am just much more captivated by and interested in the "now." Life seems effortless, though I have my recent desert chronicles to remind me, lest I forget what I went through to get here.

Time is up! So, although my heart keens to stay in the islands, I follow my itinerary, board the plane with a long sigh, and return to the desert that has been patiently awaiting my return.

May all our goings out and comings back be met with
deep breath and languid eyes. May we choose to perceive
the gifts of each change and move from place to place
with the relaxation offered through trusting life itself.

YOUR INVITATION:

1. How have geographical changes (moves or travel) mirrored what
    has been going on in your inner life (or not)?

2. How would you most like to react to unbidden change?

3. What does the place on earth where you feel most loved, vibrant,
    and whole help you to do?

THE FINAL MONTH

Chapter 17

Culturally Conditioned

During these last six months of avoiding Montana winters, I spent three in the desert and three in Hawaii. I have now returned for a final month, April, to my desert condo, wondering how the amazing journey of aloha and ocean swims with whales in the islands might affect my thoughts and feelings about my former lover—the Sonoran Desert. I move from humid waters to dry sandstone, from loving native embraces to those from my new Arizona friends and a new budding relationship with the desert itself. No surprise that April turns out to be the month where everything begins to flower; shrubs, cactus, trees, and nesting all begin in earnest. As I breathe in the fragrant smells of blooming cactus, I seek inner clues to clear out any remaining cobwebs and to heal any old misconceptions to continue to make way for the new and increasingly welcome unknown. I hope that I, too, will bloom. Maybe I am already.

One non-blooming experience I have immediately upon returning from the islands, however, is my sense of the cultural coldness of our mainland society. From the uninterested shuttle service pick-up employee, to the rude traffic, to the homeless people drifting along the sidewalks, I feel separation. Such a contrast from the warming conversations I'd have with Hawaiian taxi drivers and the smiling checkout men and women at the island grocery stores! Here in Tucson, I realize I am judging and energetically throwing separation and uncaring right back at those from whom I am not receiving love.

I breathe and self-correct. Or, in kinder terms, I self-remember. I do not pander, but I offer the respectful acknowledgment I would like to be receiving myself. Then I let it go, try to release the expectation for reciprocity, and move on. But still, it disappoints me. I am not in paradise now, where everything was effortlessly easier.

For most of my adult life, I've been on what I would term "a journey of consciousness." I have come to identify with that Inner Teacher as my constantly wise and patient guide who is both objective and kind. With its gentle nudging, I become aware daily of how I'm restricting myself or attempting to restrict, judge, or negate others, responding from an inflated or deflated ego, or acting upon unexamined beliefs, which is what I'm doing right now. I realize that treating myself or others poorly is based on my early upbringing of separation and judgment, lack of redemption, and the "need to succeed." Push others out of the way. Get there first. Be the best or do your best at any cost. How that has driven me! How it still does when I unconsciously fall into the power of my cultural conditioning! I've formed my ideas of God from limited thinking, or even chosen certain political beliefs based on a reaction against rather than a move towards something. This stops me in my tracks. Literally. I'm checking out at my familiar Tucson grocery store. Where is the love that is stronger than anything for the person in line behind me who is clearly exasperated that I'm taking too long as I return my credit card to my wallet? Will I open my heart back up as I realize this?

Recently shifting from native to mainland culture has me more aware than ever of the shadow power of cultural conditioning. But every culture also has its "upside." If the Aloha culture seems to value people over progress, my own mainland culture perhaps values invention to save time and money. But because I am so critical of it, I may not appreciate how the freedoms we enjoy are often desired and needed by other cultures. I get too busy seeing "our" shadow. Still, my own experience has shown me that true "Aloha" culture embraces and doesn't judge; it moves slower and with more ease. Mainland culture, which includes Arizona, sports a faster, materially efficient but less inclusive lifestyle. Various groups within the state are figuratively, or sometimes literally, at war with each other.

Back at the condo, fridge stocked and bags unpacked, I begin to wander around its welcome interior and flow into the outdoors and small trails I realize I've missed the past few months. But critical thoughts about mainland U.S. continue as I pick my way through bushes. As I bushwhack through tightly overgrown trees I seldom approach, I realize that the landscape is matching my overgrown mind. But, stubborn explorer that I am, I press on. We are still evolving and growing in personal as well as global awareness of all of these realizations, and that gives me hope. And, of course, with that thought (wouldn't you know it), something happens; I break through the jungle of overgrowth to a long, more accessible stretch of trail with fewer shrubs and softly undulating scenic hills. I have to chuckle: how closely the inner can match the outer! And vice-versa.

A midday breeze flits through my hair, caressing my cheeks. I pause from winding through desert shrubs, and, closing my eyes, just stand still for a while. It is then I feel trust. Trust in life and in my process. I even begin to sway with it. What if I began to court trust itself as my own dance partner? What if I remind myself that I am truly doing the best I can with my own issues, and that I "trust" that I'll keep being alerted if and as I need to change or update my understanding? My gut jolts a bit as I realize that my personal doubt and self-questioning have been culturally conditioned through my upbringing from a parent who constantly told me I was wrong, bad, and had poor motives. It created an unconscious drive to be compelled to "figure it all out" and not trust that I was sufficient as I was, able to discover and grow on my own.

Amazing, how sometimes information is revealed to us when we least expect it. That is one reason I trust the self-realization of the healed psyche: once it has released wounding and allowed the vibrant power of love to flood in, it always knows when we are open enough to learn yet another lesson in a kind and clear manner. The unhealed psyche makes negative and self-denying assumptions, but as it heals, it returns to its natural state, which is love.

Realizing this, I bend down to rest upon a sticker-free patch of dusty pink ground, literally sitting with this new awareness about the power of my own cultural and familial conditioning. It begins to sink in and carry out its loving, quiet, and inviting reconstruction while my eyes caress the mountains. The natural world, even in my new unknown relationship to the mighty desert, still provides respite and renewal, offering refreshment to my mind-weary soul. I fade into a welcomed trance, only hours later wandering back inside, hydrating while still mindlessly gazing out at the desert landscape.

End of day finds me gazing at the setting sun. Considering the welcomed sense of endings I'm feeling, it seems appropriate. Streams of reflected pinks and orange clouds linger over the western mountains just beyond my condo. For these glorious moments, I am, as Mary Oliver writes, "a bride married to amazement." I forget if I'm back in Arizona or still in the islands, and it doesn't matter. Nature lives free of our human cultural conditioning, as long as we don't ruin her with actions from unconscious values. I breathe that thought out, too, because for right now, I want to simply, as Mary Oliver also says, "…let the soft animal of my body love what it loves." So I do. Relief floods my being. I love the bright sunset colors blessing my eyes, the slight breeze so softly once again brushing past my cheek, the deep quiet and relief that sunset ushers in to my waiting heart.

Thank you for accompanying me on this journey from the islands back to the mainland. In your own inner or outer travel, may you, too, find yourself lovingly tending to your own awareness of cultural conditioning, and find that any memories that surface, when treated with tenderness, will point you in the direction of your own ultimate freedom. And may you always allow the natural world, in all her surprise and beauty, to drift into your own welcoming body.

May confidence and a healthy persistence guide us as we find our way through life with kindness and beauty, accompanied by the Grace and Ease of the natural world as our constant companions. May we consult with them frequently along the way.

YOUR INVTIATION:

1. In what way(s) has your cultural conditioning restricted you?

2. Have any positive cultural conditionings come to the rescue?

3. What assurance about all of our futures wants to live in you?

Chapter 18

Synchronicity Rising

If synchronicity is about the meaningful convergence of two or more related things, I can't imagine much connection between the arid desert and lush islands. But I am about to find out.

Upon returning to the desert, I realize that coming back to the site of my unplanned six-month quest has served as a sort of mini-rehearsal for future visits. I 've been starting over a new relationship with an old lover, but everything is different. It isn't based on a soulful, yearning, wrenching need from a life gone wrong, but instead is now relatable as I access the present, sentient wisdom and delight of the current moment. It isn't even as much a return to the former desert lover energy as it is tutored and collegial, two old cronies—the land and myself—rubbing shoulders and laughing with the wisdom bought from hard experience.

I am hardly my old self anymore.

In fact, I feel new and different each day. I have less need to feel the same and more excitement about how each new day will open. I meditate often because it keeps me awake to this partnership with life. I have moved into a kind of trust with the unknown that doesn't even question what trust is. It simply is, and I am. Being more present allows me to have a heart and mind open to each ensuing moment, uncrowded by sorrow and grief. The sorrowful past has dissolved both in the dry pink dust of the desert and the constant lapping of waves in the islands. And, now, I am freer, more often full of a quiet energy with eyes wide open to each new day. *Ah, this is change!*

As yet another dawn ensues, having awoken me to stumble out onto the back porch and align with the quiet of the new day, I feel a deep sense of satisfaction. Over the many years of my own active healing, I recovered well enough to have helped others (inhabiting the archetype of "The Wounded Healer"), and now, more fully healed, able to be even more fully present to life itself and the magical sunrises I have grown so fond of here in the Sonoran Desert. The rising sun greets the eager east faces of the many Saguaro stanchioned up the north-south running canyon. It teases the massive mountain rocks as it descends down their undulating sides, disrobing and revealing them with the adept hand of a sure lover. It reminds of the sure human lover I knew here so many years ago; I wonder if he might ever read this epistle and realize I have been referring to him. That would be a…. synchronicity? If it matched with a corresponding thought he was holding, I suppose it would.

I have seldom regularly enjoyed what I would call synchronistic events, which I refer to as "meaningful co-incidences," perhaps mostly because I have been too involved in a busy life and too busy grieving my own past to be present to the ripeness of the moment. I am just beginning to realize that synchronicities are happening all the time, all around us. We just have to focus and become aware. The act of asking (God, the Universe, whomever or whatever) to help us tune in to the present moment seems to be the key to experience the magic we so desire. Because, really, isn't that what we want when we seek it? Magic. We want to know that everything is connected and that we are a part of that matrix-like web. It seems magic to us only because we have grown so far from our original memory of that oneness. Some day we will all see it as quite normal. We might even take it for granted! What a fine day that will be.

I have been asking this grand universe to alert me to more

synchronicity in my daily life. We can all do this. The asking is to confirm in our own minds that what we are lining up with, through thought and emotion to create our future life in the present moment, is on the right track; we are in sync with the universe itself. Since I have begun a more dedicated practice of manifesting, my awareness and experience of daily synchronicity is growing, to the point that some are almost overwhelming.

As an example, three days ago, after envisioning a fabulous future that I was linking to in heart and mind, feeling the results as though they were already happening, I began thinking about how my opening to the cosmos and so much "sky" energy might be taking me away from my well-worn and cherished Native American trails of thought and practice. These wise earth teachings have been so precious to me; I didn't want to feel that I now had to ignore them in the process of my universe expanding and my perceptions changing. I wanted to incorporate all of it—earth and sky—and not have to hold them separately. I wanted to fuse these seeming opposites into my psyche and spirit.

So, while coming out of a deep meditation, I ask, *"Help me know that I am on track with this seemingly sky-oriented scientific Quantum Physics approach and that I am not ignoring my native earth teachings. Let me know if I can and perhaps already am integrating both."*

So of course, while still rocking on the back porch mid-morning, a medium-sized cat-like animal comes into view only ten yards or so to the left, deftly slinking down a narrow trail from the hill adjacent to my porch. It appears seemingly out of nowhere so suddenly that I blink in disbelief. With rounded ears, it is definitely not another bobcat. I suspend my breath, taking in information about him quickly. Whatever his species, he looks like he is a yearling, perhaps recently kicked out from Mom's care. Looking quite thin, he may be having a hard time hunting on his own although his coat is healthy, a shimmering grayish brown with leopard-like markings. But it is his eyes that are so mesmerizing. They are a completely rounded, marbled blue, large, and locked on me as he continues to slink along. Whatever his species, he is beautiful! Somehow, I remember to breathe again, taking in a gulp of air. As he silently and carefully pads even closer, never taking his eyes off mine, the thought briefly crosses my mind that he looks hungry and could potentially attack me. But my heart is too full of love and amazement to be worried.

I have stopped rocking now, suspended in time. He steps closer, his shoulder almost touching my open gate. Now he is only three feet away. I can't stop staring into his eyes, nor, it seems, he into mine. Now I am sure that he is hungry and wish I could offer him food. In "normal" reality mode, I still think he is sizing me up to see if I might *be* food. That is ok with me. I get it. But on the "miraculous" side, though I don't know quite why, I feel he is a messenger cat, a powerful animal spirit, come to bless and reassure me that, somehow, I might be on the right track with all my new quantum processes of choosing new realities.

He halts directly beside me. I have stopped breathing again, but don't care to. Or need to. It is as if the moment is breathing *me*. I send my deepest wishes to him and his own protector spirits for the food he needs to fill his belly, and then think of the dear desert rabbit he will probably kill as a result. At the same time, I envision a time in the near future where none of us will need to predate upon anything else to survive. A New Heaven and a New Earth. Don't ask me how I know this, but I know it is coming soon.

Now I take a full breath. As if the hunger I've sensed prompts him, he ever so slightly turns his head to sniff the downhill trail, lifts his shoulder, and, propelling forward, begins to amble on past me, still staring back while ever so slowly padding down along the trail that fades into the waiting shrubs. Finally, he turns away, and, without a sound, leaps lithely over a long stickered branch lying across the path, disappearing into the deep brush leading down into the cactus and mesquite-filled canyon.

I can't believe this has just happened. When I first arrived in the desert six months ago, a bobcat (a more well-known area resident) had greeted me in similar fashion, but now a …. *what?*…. has blessed me as I prepare to depart back home to Montana.

But it gets better. I go online to identify this beauty. Maybe a jaguar? There have been reports of that rare species roaming the area. But no, he was so much smaller. And there he is, in a photo, staring at me with those marble-like blue-green eyes. A young ocelot!

An ocelot, endangered, and hunted almost out of existence, now only known to exist in Texas and—you guessed it—southern Arizona. Sightings are very, very rare. Lucky me!

Now it gets even better. Looking online for "spiritual meanings of ocelot" (because of course you know I had to), it specifies: "One who is steadily connecting both the physical and spiritual realms of Earth and Sky." And, if that wasn't relevant enough, it continues: "A symbol of regeneration. The ability to move between worlds. Ability to adapt to one's surroundings. Clear vision. Connecting to and tracking the unseen."[*]

This stopped me in my own tracks. This was the answer, through synchronicity, responding to my quest for reassurance that I was on the right track between heaven and earth. It was a perfect sighting, reflecting my experience in the desert of over half a year of unplanned questing, from grieving to letting go. The human seeking and the natural world responding. Steadily connecting the physical and spiritual realms.

Still astonished, I started laughing. I couldn't erase the smile from my face. Then I grew quiet. That startled morning, my own smaller blue-green eyes, not as round, but surely as wild, stared out into the desert for a long, long time.

---

[*] *Compiled from several sources*

Synchronicity always reassures the mind
of the wisdom of the heart.

YOUR INVITATION

1. What state of awareness invites you into your own best experiences of synchronicity?

2. How might you experience more?

3. What further synchronicities might you seek as a result of this book?

EPILOGUE

I have a sense of completeness now even in the midst of the ever-changing landscape of life. You and I have spent many sunrises together and gazed at the shapes of changing light. You've been introduced to my avian and four-legged friends traveling down dry arroyos and have also, I imagine, explored your own inner terrains needing moist waters. I hope that in the process you've imbibed a template for gathering your own water for the desert, the sustenance to nourish the changes that life has brought and will continue to bring to you.

We need not be afraid. We have only to draw closer to ourselves and the intrinsic kindness of the world. We find that love is at the essence of all of life. *We do not have to create this love; our work is simply to remove the barriers to it.*

Wrestling with our consciousness, releasing resistance, and allowing realizations of how we've been asleep in our lives vastly increases self-awareness. Self-awareness intrinsically enhances self-compassion. Self-compassion then effortlessly extends itself to all others: human, animal, plant, the elements, and the universe itself.

You can and hopefully do already realize your relationship to and connection with everything. And when unbidden changes come that seem out of your control, you are invited on a very special journey. How *will* you or *do* you accept that offer? With angst and anger or with Grace and Ease?

As I review *Water for The Desert*, I see some nuggets of learned wisdom. As I age it seems more important, even urgent, to share what I've been through and what I have learned. Though perhaps like most of us, I had times I wanted to leave the planet, each time I made a conscious choice to be here, to "be here now" as spiritual teacher Ram Dass admonished. I'd seen enough ugliness. Each time I decided to still live but turn towards beauty instead. And I have been cultivating the appreciation of life ever since. I love the Navajo closing Blessing Way Ceremony prayer honoring beauty:

Walking in Beauty

In beauty I walk
With beauty before me I walk
With beauty behind me I walk
With beauty above me I walk
With beauty around me I walk
It has become beauty again.

By responding to the appealing gift of conscious awareness, life has truly become beautiful again. That of which I was unaware used to drive me, creating heartache and strife. With consciousness, it morphed into understanding, forgiveness, compassion, and letting go. It has revealed beauty everywhere. It makes me simple, in the best sense of the word. I love the inner beauty of the constant surprises offered by consciousness and realize how loved we really are. We have available spiritual experience with Ancestors, God, and Goddesses who are just waiting to respond to our open hearts and spirits. I love the outer beauty of nature, the earth, our amazing lives, all the animals and plants (well, except for spiders, ticks, and mosquitoes), and how the universe has evolved over time to become this incredible planet. I love the inner beauty of ideas and form and creativity and humor and love itself. I love the grassy breeze of summer mornings and the hushed quiet of winter evenings, the intoxication of pine forests and the sensual lapping of waves on the seashore. Don't you?

I also ache for everyone, everywhere, who suffers and is in pain or fear. On the outer plane, I do what I feel called to do to help alleviate such struggle. On the inner plane, I envision their lives and even the structure of the world itself becoming heaven on earth, and meanwhile send out love, joy, and peace. With that in mind, I leave you with these parting thoughts I am learning to absorb:

1. I can love everything through *feeling* love—cherish happiness, tend to sadness, love all of Creation.

2. I am invited to learn and use discretion, not judgment. Discretion forms when I apply wisdom; judgment is not necessary.

3. I let myself be aware of a spiritually and psychologically adept "Inner Teacher." Then I listen and respond to resulting intuition.

4. One way to love life is to focus on beauty. The more I gather it around me like a bouquet of flowers, the more I appreciate life.

5. I let myself become aware of my own shortcomings, correct mistakes wherever possible, and let alchemy transform me.

6. I choose to read or create inspiring books (or listen to podcasts) that increase my sense of sentience, connection, and wellbeing.

7. I forgive my own trespasses by applying liberal doses of self-acceptance. I also forgive myself when I am negatively existential, railing at life, God, or others. In these moments, I realize I'm feeling separate from God and can choose to instead re-connect with Source.

8. I hold strong beliefs up for spiritual inspection to be guided by new insights about them. I realize that they often change as I do.

9. I keep finding a suitable rhythm for my days and increasingly recognize the freedom I actually have to do so.

10. I love the Celtic practice of beginning a blessing with the word, "May." May everything I do flow from a full heart. May I remind myself to not do what I think I "should;" may I instead choose that which I feel lovingly guided to do.

11. I consider that I may be, and in fact am, much more powerful than I've imagined. What if we all, as aspects of God, can really and fully heal ourselves in body, mind, and spirit?

12. I keep partnering with my sense of God, allowing a deep relationship to grow and change. What can't we accomplish together?

13. I seek peace in everything I do, think, see, and say.

14. I seek increasing honesty with God/Goddess/Creator/All That Is. This includes forgiveness of self and others.

15. I'll keep storing water in the ribs of my Saguaro self so that I'll have it when the heat of change begins to burn me up. Then I will draw from a reservoir of sustenance to cool and nourish both myself and those around me.

16. YOUR INVITATION FOR ADDING YOUR OWN:

Thank you for taking this journey with me. I hope it has enhanced your own and that you will continue to find that change can be embraced, revelatory, and ultimately freeing. May your heart feel lighter, your soul deeper, and your mind freer for having accompanied me along the way. So many roads to travel. So much help to access. And so much magic to experience!

I'll be seeing you, perhaps in your next sunny or overcast day, in the next smile or tear from a passer-by, in the next moment of praise or doubt. I'll be there, too. And we'll keep morphing through all of it together. In gratitude. With Grace and Ease.

May you travel well as you increase in understanding.
May this understanding grow into kind thoughts and actions.
And may you always find comfort in the
compassionate arms of the Divine.

POSTSCRIPT

The Field of Infinite Possibilities

Is anything ever really done? Don't we always have the opportunity to change perception as we open to more in life? I can feel how I am still moving into a new consciousness. I am relieved, actually, to be leaving old ways behind, even the ones I'd so carefully carved out and by which I was so inspired. I can remember but not repeat the past, if that past has carried less love than I know now. I can release that which is old and worn as life calls me on. I can then move into vaster fields and finer ways of knowing without looking back. That is the power of the sentient divine. It beckons and we answer. I hope some of you will continue to travel with me as I write new books. Someday our eyes will meet and we'll just know one another. It might even be in that new dimension we have been intuiting.

Toward the end of this process of dissolution and resolution I morphed through, and as discussed in previous chapters, I had the great good fortune to come upon the work of several science and consciousness explorers. Reading my favorite books from Dr. Bruce Lipton (*The Biology of Belief*), Gregg Braden (*The Divine Matrix*), and Dr. Joe Dispenza (*You Are the Placebo* and *Becoming Supernatural*), I see why they jokingly refer to themselves as the "Three Amigos;" they share a good-natured comradeship while each brilliantly carving out their own piece of the quantum physics pie and making it deliciously digestible to the lay person. They also all agree that without activating our heart center, we will not manifest our hearts' desires, including creating a better world. Their work is compatible with all the teachers of compassion I have known; the outcome shines in the lives of those who have been awakened by it. We have so many teachers, even life itself.

While it has taken me years to understand what many bright intellects surely absorb more quickly, what each of the Three Amigos' works opens in my mind and heart is how miraculous the universe is and how much more we can be constantly actualizing our true potential. The way cells heal in our bodies through heart-inspired thought, the manifesting action of wave into particle, and the proof of the interconnectedness of all things excite my broader mind, moving me into that "field of all possibilities." We have so many opportunities to awaken to the ancient ability to heal ourselves of physical and emotional pain, to live in the bounty of the present moment, and to create lives filled with wonder, synchronicities, and abundance.

This is not New Age fluff. It is supported by scientific tenants drawn from ongoing discoveries of our innate but sometimes dormant capabilities. Even studies of the neurobiology of consciousness research exploring where consciousness might physically dwell has given rise to gatherings such as the annual international "Science and Consciousness" conference, held in Tucson every other year. Although presenters or attendees might conduct heated debates, it is heartening that so much interest and intrigue about the topic is being researched. As science keeps re-defining itself and gains more momentum in connecting the human mind and heart, we might also find a bit of redemption for some New Age approaches, which have tended to favor intuition over science. Thanks to so many consciousness explorers, we are beginning to close the gap between science and intuition. Leaning more toward intuition myself, it is a great relief to see this happening. Science is "proving" what I have known (or suspected) all along! I love the bridge they have created.

But even my fascination with Quantum Physics may well change in my perspective or priorities over time. Although I imagine I'll keep building on all that I learn, what matters to me today may not matter so much tomorrow, or next year, or in the next lifetime. All I can do is be as present and honest as possible to my truth in the moment, which is what I have sought to do here. And doing so with compassion will likely never eclipse itself. As I smile, and even chuckle a bit, my buoyant and adventurous inner child concurs. She is sure I will never die and will also take her with me wherever I go. I nod. Of course. Where would I be without her?

As I write, life continues to sing around me. A brown and tan bird with a long beak is chortling on a tall ocotillo branch out my back porch. I rock a few more times on my chair before leaving my desert retreat, glancing one more time at my avian friend calling out as his branch sways in the light morning breeze. He keeps his balance while he looks around, seeming to listen to the other birds around him. He is there, and alive, and now he flies away. I am no less for his absence, but love seeing him close, too. Could we live our lives this way? Enchanted by beauty without feeling lack? Knowing that we are the beauty, too? And that we could even give *that* away for the experience of a broader field where we could realize beauty in a vaster way, even the beauty of the unknown?

The body chills I got just now concur. I am here and more than here. A Cactus Wren jumps into the cradling arms of the Saguaro just outside my porch gate, looking down its interior to something I can't see. I have to wander closer, standing on my tiptoes to catch a glimpse. Beautiful! A nest in progress! New life. And so it goes. I envision this beauty morphing into a wider knowing, a more miraculous way of being, perhaps one that leads to heaven on earth, where nothing suffers and nothing predates upon anything else. That is my ongoing vision, to allow all we learn to catapult us into the ability to live in that field of possibilities, particle and wave that we are, and realize that life is so much more than we have thought it to be.

That said, here we are still reeling in a world that is crumbling and full of toxic chemicals, people, and actions. It won't take long in the coming days for me to realize more: that I have held onto the past without realizing it, that it has not occurred to me to allow Grace and Ease to arise right through the middle of suffering, and that I have denigrated the difficult, wanting to accept only the beautiful. This reaction is understandable from a life too full of difficulty, but still, aren't most lives that way? I can allow deep disappointment, anger, sorrow, or whatever troubling emotions arise to prompt me to further envision and manifest that which is more desirable. At the same time, I can embrace perceived dark and light, seeming opposites of indifference and compassion. For me, this is big: everything, in fact. Is this blending of opposites, led by love itself, the leading edge of alchemical, evolutionary change? I know it is my own.

A deep breath emanates from within. I move from the macrocosm of the big picture to the microcosm of my own small life; I breathe, walk indoors, gulp a glass of water, inhale deeply, and feel relief flowing through, like the soul being revived, like water for the desert, like nourishing all the places that thirst.

While indoors, I take one last look out the corner windows to the desert that has morphed from encompassing lover to gentle backdrop. A humming bird alights on a swaying ocotillo branch as a wren alights on another one from the same plant. The ocotillo is attracting them by sporting its long orangey-red blossoms in a messy and delightful way. I love messes in nature. Can I love my own messes? Could they, too, have been and still be beautiful, and can I perhaps even allow myself to change the perception that anything is a mess at all; that "messes" are perhaps just wild explosions of life, as is my own, not tight little squares with neat corners? Fabulous, arcing, curling explosions into the world that we have all had a hand at creating?

I am a work in progress; I do not know where my awareness will be next week or next year or whenever I leave this life. Or how it might change in the next life. As I gently let go of further thought, I open into the whoosh of a greater unknown, now eager to discover what is waiting. I trust it will be fruitful, and ultimately, good.

I am aware of the divine now in a non-egoic way and can claim, *"Yes, I helped create all this beauty, too. The mind and heart of God is in me, filtered through my human challenges, awareness, and unique possibilities. I am here and also there, now and then, yesterday, today and tomorrow. I am all things; all possibilities live in me."*

All this gleaned from gazing out at this verdant desert full of so many surprises, a wave from the Field morphed into particles of living perception. Particles, blinking in and out. I can also be here, plain and simple little earth girl that I am, and "there," disappearing into the invisible wave of the divine and flying beyond the speed of light around the heart of the universe. What a gift beyond words for me, who loves language, to be realizing its power, and my own, all at the same time. I keep stretching my arms wider to embrace it all. I believe I will always thirst, trusting that with my remaining years in this body I will keep finding new sources of water and new ways of storing it. And like the Saguaro, when I 'drop my robes' (as my native friends say) and my ribs lie open and exposed, they will provide a place for others to still thrive on the sustenance I have gleaned. *If* I die. (You know who had me write that.)

Life is good.

May we all experience the magic, majesty, and inter-connectedness of the world in all its forms today, including our own selves. May we be fully present, opening always to a wider knowing, a deeper truth, and more magnificent lives. And may we lovingly invite everyone and everything along as we leap into this increasingly welcomed unknown journey that we can know together!

ACKNOWLEDGEMENTS

A book is always the result of a community of participants. I am grateful for both the long-standing team who have guided and supported my writings for many years now as well as new ones who always seem to come along just when needed.

With gratitude to my writer's group, as always: Barbara McGowan, artist and author of *A Brush With Nature*, and Ginny Watts, performer and author of an upcoming book exploring dance as a spiritual practice. Their perusal of my work and insightful suggestions always round out my offerings. Among the many others who read and gave valuable feedback on selected chapters of *Water For The Desert* are: Margie Chase, Steve Guettermann, Jeff Jackson, Marta Bush, Romel Trubee, and Lisa Featherstone. Their thoughtful comments deepened my own insights. Also, authors and consciousness explorers Joe Dispensa, Gregg Braden, and Bruce Lipton continue to inspire and enliven my work, as do the Abraham teachings, Depak Chopra, the principles of Transpersonal Psychology, the offerings of the Institute of Noetic Sciences, David Whyte, John O'Donahue, Bill Plotkin, Angeles Arrien, David Abram, and the musical magic of Solfeggio.

My thanks also to Balboa and their conscientious efforts to help this book be published within a good timeframe, and to my awesome editor, Kate McGunagle, whose Princeton and Oxford education shone through at every step. She helped make the whole publishing process easy!

And last but not least, I offer reams of gratitude to Spirit, the universal life force that breathes through all of us, no matter what name we give it. I am forever grateful for Life itself and the power of Consciousness to help us re-balance, recover health, and thrive.